Hang in There, Girl

Hang in There, Girl

Cally Logan

BRIDGE LOGOS

Newberry, FL 32669

Bridge-Logos
Newberry, FL 32669

Hang in There, Girl:
Real-Life Advice from a Big Sister in Christ
by Cally Logan

Printed in the United States of America

Library of Congress Catalog Card Number: 2021950442

International Standard Book Number: 978-1-61036-271-9

Edited by Lynn Copeland

Cover and interior design by Kent Jensen | knail.com

VP 1/12/2022

To my grandfather Ben Blanton Sr.
and the legacy he planted long ago.

And most truly,
all honor, glory, and praise to Jesus Christ,
to whom all credit is due.

CONTENTS

INTRODUCTION

Hi there.

Coming of age in this world is harder than ever, and more often than not we find ourselves needing a big sister in life. The kind of big sister you could ask embarrassing or hard questions of, the kind who would offer godly advice from a genuine desire to help. One who would offer what we *need* to hear more than what we *want* to hear. Although I do not know you personally, I hope this book serves as a "coffee date" with a big sister in Christ. Imagine us nestled into worn, cozy leather chairs in the corner of a local coffee shop, with a leisurely afternoon ahead of us just to chat.

Matthew 10 shares how God knows every sparrow, and reader, He knows you. I hope as you read through this book it feels like a comforting hug—warm and embracing, but never judgmental. Rest assured that the chapters to come have been heavily prayed over and ample time in the Word has been spent upon these revelations and convictions. You see, it is really the Holy Spirit of God prompting me to write. I say this because in this world we need to be discerning. If we are going to take time to listen to people, we need to know that they are biblically sound. This requires the correct balance of Scripture and Spirit, and that is something I adamantly pursue, especially in this book.

So, hang in there, girl, you're not alone in this life. Pour yourself a fresh cup and let's have a little chat about growing up, growing in, and having life abundantly.

CHAPTER 1

Radical

LIVE RAD

What does it really mean to be a Christian? What is the difference between a cultural Christian and a true follower of Christ? The answer is how you choose to live out your life. A cultural Christian is someone who has merely accepted into their hearts and minds that Jesus is the Son of God, but a genuine follower of Christ has also turned from their sin and chooses daily to live out a life imitating Christ. This means living in such a way that people can tell you are set apart; you are living as Christ called all of us to live. This is represented most by how we love, as Jesus said: "By this everyone will know that you are my disciples, if you love one another" (John 13:35).

Now, even those who are not followers of Christ can love someone else. Love is best defined as putting another person before ourselves. What if we radically took that to the next level? To a Christ-follower level? What if we chose to not live in even the mainstream of church culture, but we actually lived as Christ did?

This would require stepping out of our comfort zones. Suddenly keeping to our safe Christian circles of friends would be challenged as we choose to sit with people who aren't saved, people who don't live perfectly, even the outcasts. Jesus did this plain and simple, such as the time He chose to sit with tax collectors (unpopular in any time) and even women who sold themselves for money. Now, what is important is to realize that Jesus never said what they did was acceptable, nor did He participate in their sins, yet He radically loved and accepted them as people who needed to know the love of God. How can we imitate Christ in this? Perhaps we can sit with that coworker who always sits alone at lunch. Perhaps we can start up a conversation with someone who doesn't look a thing like us. Perhaps we can love radically.

For many people, fitting in is a great desire, but I've always felt comfortable walking to a unique beat all my own. That being said, my "people" are usually those who perk up at the mention of *Lord of the Rings*, a historical event, or a pop-punk band of the early 2000s. I honestly would not change a thing about myself in that manner, for it allows me to connect and engage with others on many levels and provides the blessing and opportunity to love them. It honestly breaks my heart seeing what a skewed and wrong perception most people have about Christians. From movies to television to culture, there seems to be the narrative that Christians are judgmental, self-righteous, and unwilling to come alongside the least of these, and changing that stereotype falls upon us in action.

Gandhi said, "I know of no one who has done more for humanity than Jesus. In fact, there is nothing wrong with Christianity, but the trouble is with you Christians. You do not begin to live up to your own teachings,"[1] and that vividly spoke to me. I am in no way bashing church culture, but it is time we break the mold and stereotype that Christians are bigots who judge others and misrepresent the name of Christ. It is time we step out and live radically just as Jesus did. It is time we love others and embrace them in love, not condemning or affirming their actions, but merely loving them as individuals made in God's image.

Living radically also means we live differently than society, and even church culture. We uphold what Christ calls us to do, like keeping Sundays holy and tithing. It means waiting to have sex until marriage, and placing a high value on marriage in the first place. It means picking up our cross and following His lead, even if it looks dangerous and terrifying. Christ never once said that He would call us to live in secure little bubbles on Comfort Zone Island. He called us to trust Him and be different.

Our society oddly enough often highlights how great it is to be different, so what if we actually lived like Jesus calls us to live? What if we took the first ten minutes of our mornings and read the Word, and His own words, rather than scroll through Instagram? What if we didn't conform to the ways of this world but instead wholly ran after Him, not worrying about our reputations or the thoughts of others but truly just caring about what *He* thinks of us? What if we lived radically and pursued a life after Him? What if we turned these "what ifs" into actions and actually did them? That is what this book is about. Learning and striving to live radically different from what society and even misguided Pharisees of church culture demand, and choosing to pick up your cross and follow Christ daily, as Jesus said: "If anyone would come after me, he must deny himself and take up his cross daily and follow me" (Luke 9:23).

So, I ask you, are you ready?

Prayer

Dear Lord,
Thank You. Thank You for giving us such a beautiful
example of how to live and how we can best serve You. Lord,
please ever mold our hearts to Your desires and Your will, so that
we may live in such an abundance. Please guide our hearts to be
steadfast and radically bold, stepping out to not merely confess You
as Lord, but to take up our own crosses and follow You.
In Your name,
Amen.

WHO IS GOD?

When I was a teen my youth director said something that has stuck with me for over a decade: "If you are going to spend all of eternity with God, shouldn't you know more of who He is?" This hit me like a punch to the gut, though I did not fully understand it until later. It's a continuous process. As Christians we can get so stuck on desiring to know the will of God, but wouldn't it be easier to understand His will if we understood more of who He is?

The Bible is our only source of absolute truth, and in this God-breathed Word we can find answers to all of life's questions as He speaks to us through a verse or story. The Bible has much to share on the character of God; these verses give us just a glimpse of who He is:

- "Jesus Christ is the same yesterday and today and forever" (Hebrews 13:8).
- "Whoever who does not love does not know God, because God is love" (1 John 4:8).

- "But ask the animals, and they will teach you, or the birds of the air, and they will tell you; or speak to the earth, and it will teach you, or let the fish of the sea inform you. Which of all these does not know that the hand of the LORD has done this? In his hand is the life of every creature and the breath of all mankind" (Job 12:7–10).
- "I am the true vine, and my Father is the vinedresser. He cuts off every branch in me that bears no fruit, while every branch that does bear fruit he prunes so that it will be even more fruitful. You are already clean because of the word I have spoken to you. Remain in me, and I will remain in you. No branch can bear fruit by itself; it must remain in the vine. Neither can you bear fruit unless you remain in me. I am the vine; you are the branches. If a man remains in me and I in him, he will bear much fruit; apart from me you can do nothing" (John 15:1–5).
- "He who is the Glory of Israel does not lie or change his mind; for he is not a man, that he should change his mind" (1 Samuel 15:29).

From just a glimpse of these few verses the truth we don't even begin to scratch the surface of God. He is infinite and omnipotent, He is everywhere and over every single thing, but in seeking Him more deeply, we can come to know Him through our lives. One of the most important verses listed above is the last one telling us that God is not a man that He should lie or change His mind. This is evident through many stories of women in the Bible.

Hannah, the mother of the prophet Samuel, saw firsthand the character of God through an answer to prayer (see 1 Samuel 1). She was barren and ashamed, and desperately desired a child to bless her husband, but also to honor God at the same time (v. 11).

The Bible states that Hannah wept bitterly as she desperately prayed. Through the prayer of her husband, Elkanah, God blessed her in granting her request, giving her hope that her desire would be fulfilled. That is the key—God moved on her behalf. To a woman literally mocked for being barren, He honored her request for a child. Hannah rejoiced in this. Not merely because she saw the fulfillment of her aching heart literally born through a child, but because she knew with no shadow or hint of doubt that the God she served was compassionate, loving, merciful, and cared about her. She could stand all the days of her life knowing full well that her God was faithful. Her prayer to the Lord in thanksgiving is incredible:

> "My heart rejoices in the LORD; in the LORD my horn is lifted high. My mouth boasts over my enemies, for I delight in your deliverance. There is no one holy like the LORD; there is no one besides you; there is no Rock like our God." (1 Samuel 2:1–2)

This is a woman who knows who her God is. Now the caveat to this is that there were seasons that were rough for her. Coming to know the true character of God more often than not requires seasons in which we encounter various issues, and trust must be built and made in Him. Thousands of years later we can draw hope and inspiration from her story, but we would not know her journey had the circumstances been different. Her miracle story held such meaning because of the struggle that came before. For others in the Bible and beyond, the story may be a promise, or it may be a problem. The glorious thing about God is that He is never changing, so all that is true for those in the Bible times is true for us today.

John shares in the final chapter of his Gospel that if he were to share all that Christ had done on this earth, we could never finish reading about them. "Jesus did many other things as well. If every one of them were written down, I suppose that even the whole world would not have room for the books that would be written" (John 21:25). We serve an unchanging God, so do not believe for one second that we forfeit anything just because we don't live in the years the Bible was recorded.

Another mighty woman whose trust in God led to her fulfillment and discovery of His true character was Elizabeth. She was the mother of John the Baptist. Elizabeth was well beyond childbearing years, but in answer to her husband's prayers, the Lord sent an angel to Zechariah to tell him that they would have a son. Rendered unable to speak until the child was born, Zechariah no doubt shared the news with his wife in writing (see Luke 1:60–63). Elizabeth believed the angel's promise and held firm to it. In due time, she and Zachariah did indeed conceive a child. Later she comes to find that she is not alone is receiving a gift from God. She exclaims to her cousin Mary, "Blessed is she who has believed that what the Lord has said to her will be accomplished!" (Luke 1:45). When she said this, it was to encourage Mary. Mary, the mother of Christ...

Let's take a moment to allow that to completely sink in. God showed His true character in fulfilling a promise to a couple, and the woman who carried the promise was then used to encourage the mother of Christ in her own promise. That is what fellowship is—encouraging one another in Christ about who He is. D. T. Niles says, "Christianity is one beggar telling another beggar where he found bread."

To bring this back around, let us seek Him. Let us seek Him to find Him and to know Him well. In Matthew 7:7 Jesus says, "Ask and it will be given to you; seek and you will find; knock and the door will be opened to you." The fact of the matter is that, though promises given to the women mentioned here and to others through the span of history were fulfilled, they are merely bonuses in reality. The greatest and most glorious gift of all is knowing more deeply who the Creator truly is, His faithfulness, and His never-ending love. The greatest blessing of all time is knowing and standing upon such future promises and His past faithfulness so that, no matter what may befall us in life, we have a firm and secure anchor in knowing who He is and that all things are woven together for His glory and our benefit. Let us rejoice in that promise of Romans 8:28 and indeed go forth to seek Him, asking Him to reveal His character to us. After all, if we are to spend all of eternity with Him, we should know Him as well as we can.

Prayer

Dear Lord Jesus,
Thank You for Your enduring and loving grace. We pray that
during the trials and lessons we learn throughout our lives that
You would be glorified through Your constant faithfulness and
mercy. We pray that You would anchor us and work deeply in us
so that we could come to know You better. We pray that, just as
Elizabeth saw Your glory manifested in a fulfilled promise, we
would not shy away from circumstances where You would provide
for such great promises, such great faith, and such great miracles.
In Your name,
Amen.

BUILD YOUR RELATIONSHIP

When I was little, my plan was to marry young and start having children early on. As time would prove, that hope was answered with the challenge to not only wait, but to trust Him in the wait. God has a habit of growing His children during seasons of waiting. Consider Abraham, who was called to trust God for the promise of a family, and to trust that the answer of "wait" was sufficient. God knew what was best. You see, God had bigger plans for Abraham, just as He had bigger plans for me than I even had for myself. His plans for me came about from building my relationship with God while I was single.

The goal of a relationship with God is not at all to be given a spouse as a gift, but a marriage will be more blessed by having a deeper relationship with God. The more we seek His face, the more we find the living water that satisfies our souls. Jeremiah 33:3 says, "Call to me and I will answer you and tell you great and unsearchable things you do not know." Our lives are marked by great unknowns and questions that we frequently ponder, yet more often than not we rely too heavily on our own strengths to find them out. More often than not, we end up with even more questions and fewer answers.

Society has taught us that to be functional adults we must be completely self-sufficient and reliant upon our own strengths, yet that only yields a perfectionist complex marked with overwhelming impossibilities to actually live up to such a demand. We buy into the lie that everyone else has their act together, and we are the only ones who don't. We buy into the lie that somehow we are the only ones insecure on this planet. What if for even just a few minutes we took off the facade that we can succeed in life by ourselves and realized our deep need for a Savior—not only for our eternity but for our day-to-day? Christ wants to take on what weighs us down, and He wants to walk with you in your life. Not just through the milestones but every single step. I kid you not, I sometimes even ask Him to direct the hairdresser when I get my hair colored!

Jesus tells us, "Come to me, all you who are weary and burdened, and I will give you rest" (Matthew 11:28). What Jesus is saying here is that He actually wants your burdens—your good, your bad, your ugly. He wants to walk this path with you, and eventually work even the bad and ugly things out for your favor. The thing is, that takes a real relationship with Him.

I've come to hate the correlation of being a follower of Christ with the word "religion." The dictionary defines religion as "a set of beliefs concerning the cause, nature, and purpose of the universe, especially when considered as the creation of a superhuman agency or agencies, usually involving devotional and ritual observances, and often containing a moral code governing the conduct of human affairs."[2] Religion will tell you what to do to make yourself "right" with God, when to do it, and how to do it, and if you mess up, how to atone for your sin. Beyond that, you're alone in a vast universe with no real crutch or friend to rely on.

Being a follower of Christ entails a relationship with Him, built on His faithfulness and His love. You in turn find yourself wanting to follow the laws in the Bible, because of that love found in Christ. It isn't out of guilt that you are dutiful, it is out of love for God. More so, when you do fail to meet expectations as you will as a human, He freely forgives you. Because of the relationship aspect, you don't want to do it again, because you don't want to let Him down again. That is unlike any "religion" or collective practice any human could ever possibly dream up.

So how does one really dig in and deepen a relationship with God? For those who are completely new to even knowing God, how can they start such a relationship? It begins with honest and vulnerable prayer. The kind of prayer where you come before Him with reverence and respect, but you are raw, honest, and real with Him. He knows everything about you anyway; you won't surprise Him with anything He doesn't already know. What comes next is getting to know Him through His Book, the Bible. The apostle John writes, "In the beginning was the Word, and the Word was with God, and the Word was God. He was with God in the beginning. Through him all things were made; without him nothing was made that has been made. In him was life, and that life was the light of men. The light shines in the darkness, but the darkness has not understood it" (John 1:1–5). We can come to know Him better by reading His breathed Word. This Word is something of the utmost value, for in our hands we can tangibly hold the only absolute moral truth on the planet. In this Word, we can come to know His character, faithfulness, miracles, and love. The Bible is the sole book the reader can pick up and feel loved by the Author.

Community comes into play next. As followers of Christ, we are collectively His body, the church (see Ephesians 5:23). We are called to meet together, worship together, share burdens and blessings together, and work together as a team for Him. Prayerfully seeking a good Bible-based church is vital to deepening your relationship with God. God will often use His children to speak to you. The pertinent thing here is to get into a church that is solidly rooted in the Word and the truth.

Most of all, we build our relationship with God in the day-to-day activities. Paul calls for believers to "pray continually" (1 Thessalonians 5:17). This can be difficult at first, but when put into practice will become as natural as breathing. Anytime you find yourself with a free thought, pray it out. Talk to God about that person at school or work who was bothering you. Talk to Him about how to handle friends, guys, your parents. Your greatest and strongest relationship should be with God, and like all relationships, that requires getting to know the other person through communication. He will speak to you in an abundance of ways; you just have to listen.

So, work on your relationship with Him now when you are young, for when life gets harder, or when the issues get bigger, you'll have Him right there with you.

Prayer

Dear Lord,
We thank You for Your love and for who You are.
We pray that You would overwhelm us with Your enduring
and loving Holy Spirit. We invite you in this very moment into
our lives, hearts, circumstances, and days. We pray that Your
love would cover us like a fresh blanket of snow, not leaving even
a fragment of our lives untouched by You. We pray for a deeper
knowledge and relationship with You, so that we may come to
know You better on this side of the veil.
In Jesus' name we pray,
Amen.

LEARNING TO TRUST

How often do we say to others, "I trust God," when in all truthfulness we are scared out of our minds? Though we are holding on to hope that He will meet our needs, we are beginning to lay up bricks to create walls around our hearts, separating us from God, because we think there is a chance that He won't actually come through. I think it's about time that we become honest with ourselves and with God and say, "I'm learning to trust You, God." This is honest, and it is okay to say. He knows it, and honestly a deeper relationship can be formed when we are honest with Him rather than putting up facades blockading the truth.

C. S. Lewis said, "We are not necessarily doubting that God will do the best for us; we are wondering how painful the best will turn out to be."[3] Or, for a more musical take, Relient K wrote in their song, "Let It All Out":

And you said I know that this will hurt
But if I don't break your heart then things will just get worse
If the burden seems too much to bear
Remember the end will justify the pain it took to get
  us there.[4]

When God calls us to do a mission or task, it is rarely without endurance and pain. We tend to doubt His goodness and His love and fall into not trusting Him when those challenges spring up in front of us. Lack of trust comes from fear. This is why it is good to be honest with God during these times when we don't trust Him. One of the greatest biblical examples of this can be seen when Jesus calms the storm:

> That day when evening came, he said to his disciples, "Let us go over to the other side." Leaving the crowd behind, they took him along, just as he was, in the boat. There were also other boats with him. A furious squall came up, and the waves broke over the boat, so that it was nearly swamped. Jesus was in the stern, sleeping on a cushion. The disciples woke him and said to him, "Teacher, don't you care if we drown?"
>
> He got up, rebuked the wind and said to the waves, "Quiet! Be still!" Then the wind died down and it was completely calm.
>
> He said to his disciples, "Why are you so afraid? Do you still have no faith?"
>
> They were terrified and asked each other, "Who is this? Even the wind and the waves obey him!" (Mark 4:35–41)

Even Jesus' disciples were terrified and did not trust Him in this example. Recall here that these men had seen countless healings, miracles, and wonders while following Him. Many of them were also skilled fishermen, so the seas were nothing new to them, but this was one whopper of a storm. They glanced over to see Jesus sleeping, unafraid and unbothered by the winds, yet they ran around like chickens with their heads cut off. They didn't trust Him for those moments. They finally woke Jesus up and begged Him to save them, and He responded, "Do you still have no faith?" We can relate to the disciples here. So often we get caught up in the storms that we don't actually trust Him to get us to the other side.

So, what do we do? Do we side idly during the storms and ignore them? Or do we actually admit that we are learning to trust God and leave it there at the cross? Being honest with God is exactly what we need to do. None of us are perfect; if we were and had spotless faith, what would be the real need for a Savior? If we could save ourselves, why then would we need to put our faith in an omnipotent God? In no way am I saying that through every storm we will doubt and lose faith or trust, but it is okay to be learning throughout. Storms build endurance, so over time we become stronger in Him. Suddenly what was a hurricane in the past is now nothing more than a drizzling shower. The key is that we are learning, just as the disciples were learning. We are learning to trust God and learning more about His character with each passing day. We are learning that we are flawed humans in desperate need of a Savior, and we are learning that He doesn't just love us, He actually likes us and has what's best for us in store.

Prayer

Dear Lord,
You know our hearts and minds. Help us to be more honest
and vulnerable with You, so that we may come into a deeper
relationship with You. Please teach us more of Your character to
help us grow in our faith in You, so that when storms come we
may not fear and we may develop a greater trust in You.

We love You and earnestly desire to trust and not fear,
but when our faith has holes, please work in us to fill them. Please
bring us into a deeper understanding of You and Your plans for
us that glorify You and benefit us.
In Jesus' name,
Amen.

SURRENDER

There is a common fallacy that we allow our prideful flesh to buy into—that "surrender" is death. In reality, it is, but perhaps not all death is a bad thing. Perhaps death to self can actually be the key that unlocks truly living. Stick with me now…

When we are young, society tells us that the only way to success and happiness is to be independent. We live in a country literally built on the concept of independence, and the American Dream is in itself self-sufficiency and self-reliance. Being independent is not completely a bad thing; after all, we do not want to remain in an infant state needing someone else to clean up our messes and perform everything for us. On the other hand, complete independence is a date with loneliness, which in time can create a feeling of cynical isolation. The concept of the world resting on our shoulders with no one to help support it will only cause us to crumble. This is why we need a relationship with our Creator. We need a Savior. It is plain and simple, really: we need Someone who knows far more than we do to help direct our paths and kiss our boo-boos at times. We need Someone who knows us intimately and yet still loves us. We need Jesus. But in this need for Jesus we must die to ourselves. Romans 8:13 says, "For if you live according to the sinful nature, you will die; but if by the Spirit you put to death the misdeeds of the body, you will live." Likewise, Jesus says, "If anyone would come after me, he must deny himself and take up his cross daily and follow me. For whoever wants to save his life will lose it, but whoever loses his life for me will save it" (Luke 9:23–24).

In dying to our flesh, we are actually allowing the Spirit within us to have complete control. When we stop fearing this death, we stop fearing real life. We will truly live, and we have the assurance that Jesus has our back. Isaiah 48:17 says, "I am the LORD your God, who teaches you what is best for you, who directs you in the way you should go." When we seek God, He actually has our best in mind. When we die to our own wills and selfish ambitions, He blesses us. Think of how Psalm 37:4 puts it: "Delight yourself in the LORD and he will give you the desires of your heart." The pertinent piece of that verse is that when we delight in Him and allow Him to move in our hearts, He can plant seeds of hope. He fulfills His will in us so those seeds will grow and prosper; you will not only be blessed with that fruit, but your relationship with Him will become your true delight. God tells us, "Those who hope in me will not be disappointed" (Isaiah 49:23).

This isn't to say that dying to yourself and delighting in the Lord are a straight shot to blessings and joy. In reality, the path is often extremely steep and hard. Rather, it means that in the end you won't be disappointed. In the end that surrender will bring you to the truest and purest joy and happiness, which is Christ Himself. John Piper coined it well: "He is most glorified when we are most satisfied in Him." We won't be disappointed when we are walking in highest satisfaction in Him. This the immeasurably glorious joy doesn't come from the "stuff" He gives us, but from loving Him *and* being loved in return. Suddenly even the long and tedious paths He calls us to become worth it. Suddenly the letdowns of the flesh become meaningless. Suddenly the blessings become icing on the cake, but the true reward and the true substance is God. He is our reward, He is our delight, and He is what makes all of life's hardships worth it.

As God's kids, we are children of the King and are therefore royalty. Have you thought of yourself that way? Of course, royal children do have perks, benefits, and blessings that are vastly different from what those who are not royal receive. The children are given favorable gifts, have the direct ear of the King, and have a relationship and exclusive time with the King that those who are not His do not have. Yet, members of royalty are also held to a higher standard. As ambassadors representing the Kingdom as a whole, they are therefore expected to live differently. This means, in the case of the Kingdom of God, living by the encouragement and ways of the Word, not by the ways of the world. Yet consider how knowing you are royalty would make obedience a great joy, for you have the honor, the pleasure, and the blessing to live out a life worthy of your calling.

So perhaps surrender isn't a bad thing after all. Perhaps it is in surrender that we truly find what it is to live and be happy. In my personal experience, it is only when I surrender something at the cross completely (and typically after soaking it in tears) that the clearest answers flood back. God delights in doing good for His kids, and I hope, dear reader, that you are counted in that group. Maybe that white flag is just the thing we need to signify that we are indeed ready to be made clean at last.

Dear Lord,
Thank You for being a God who waits for us patiently,
but also a God who helps us to know when we need to surrender.
Help us, Lord, to give control of our lives to You. Help us
to put down our own selfish pride and rest in
the drenching grace that is Your Holy Spirit.
In Jesus' name,
Amen.

CHAPTER 2

Mirror, Mirror

DON'T COMPARE WHERE YOU ARE TO OTHERS

We all have heard the idiom, "Comparison is a thief of joy," and while it is indeed true, it can be a struggle not to judge your season in life against that of your peers. I am the last of my friend group who is still single. My closest friend in Minnesota just welcomed the arrival of a precious little boy last month, and my best friend in Richmond will likely be engaged before this book is published. There have been times when I felt guilty in my *longing* to have a husband and children. Satan has a way of manipulating us to either covet or collapse into a puddle of guilt for desiring. The latter is not a place of jealousy, rather just an authentic yearning for something. The enemy will attempt to make us want to conceal or deny that ache, but recall Proverbs 13:12: "Hope deferred makes the heart sick, but a longing fulfilled is a tree of life." That seed of hope is not something to be ashamed of but something to pray over and tend, trusting God as the Master Gardener. Believe it or not, it's okay not to be where all your friends are at the moment.

Society encourages comparison and competition; it is literally rooted into the bedrock of every aspect of our culture. It is not just a matter of who walks down the aisle first, but who has the more thriving career path, or who has children first, and from there it only continues into more and more comparison. So, if we are continuing on the path of radically and authentically following Christ, what does that look like for us individually? How can we continue to hang in there when it feels like we are being left behind?

There's a chance you're like my friend Charlotte, climbing that incredible corporate ladder and reaching amazing career goals. Or perhaps you're like my friend Nicole, who married right out of college and has a beautiful son. Or perhaps you are like me, still waiting and trusting in my later twenties for God to bring a mate. More than anything, I am trusting that the work being done within me in the meantime holds just as much importance, if not more, than the change of my last name. We all have different stories, but there is something kind of amazing about that. Romans 8:28 is a classic coffee mug verse, but that doesn't make it any less true. It states, "And we know that in all things God works for the good of those who love him, who have been called according to his purpose." But what does this mean for you?

Romans 8:28 honestly could be the tagline of the entire Bible. That or John 13:7 where Jesus said, "You do not realize now what I am doing, but later you will understand." Both verses share the truth that we do not understand why things are the way they are for us, yet our circumstances are in fact an incredible blessing. Jeremiah 1:5 shares, "Before I formed you in the womb I knew you, before you were born I set you apart."

God knows what He is doing in your life, because every single day was planned before you even came to be. Isn't that a comfort?

The days we spend crying alone in the corner of our closets or screaming at Him in the parking lot of the gym are constructive because we are pressing harder into Him, and He sees the whole picture. He sees the beginning and the end. As cliché as it sounds, that expression, "When everything is falling apart, it is actually falling together," is true. He has a plan for all the good and bad to work out for your benefit, and even better, for His glory.

People tend to put on masks pretending that everything is perfect and amazing, while deep down they are screaming over something not being great. Life will never be perfect, but we can come to a point of gratitude every day for the things that are right in life. On some days it's harder than others to find this joy, but it is possible. For me, I long to be a wife and mother, to wear cute little sundresses, make pies for my husband, and play outside with my kids watching clouds every day. Instead, for now I am working as a school teacher and am making those pies and treats for my parents. That is no less glorifying to Him, for I know this is where God has me for today. Where you are right now is where God ordained for you to be, and it is where you can serve Him best in this moment.

It becomes easy to compare ourselves with one another in a world with so much social media. I won't be one of those authors who gets up on a soapbox to condemn social media for its perfectionist flaws, but it does create a facade of reality. That picture-perfect moment was probably one of fifty selfies taken with frowns in between. Girls always suck in before a picture for a more svelte figure, and aim for the perfect angle to try to look like Kim K. Perhaps if we spend less time comparing ourselves to each other, and more time being real and raw, we could finally get somewhere. That human element would finally shine through and we could all agree that we are broken humans, imperfect in every way, and so desperately in need of love and acceptance. Isn't that the heart of every human anyway—desiring to be wanted and loved? And isn't that the mission of Christ Himself—to call you home to be wanted and loved by God and to not walk alone?

Wherever you are today is right where it is best for you. Believe it or not, that job you're hating in retail will one day prepare you for your next job and the job after that. This hard season will prepare you for bigger challenges to come later on, and that endurance muscle you've built will come to totally crush the little obstacles ahead. Where you are right now may seem like a total mountain to climb, but He knows how to get you to the top, and He knows how to train you as well. Know that He loves and cares for you, and He will guide you in the best way to go. Remember Proverbs 3:5–6 when in doubt: "Trust in the LORD with all your heart and lean not on your own understanding. In all your ways acknowledge him, and he will make your paths straight."

Prayer

Dear Lord,
Thank You for the fact that, like snowflakes, we are all uniquely made by You. Lord, we pray that as we each live out our lives we do not fall into the pit of comparison. Just as You never healed two people in the same way, You write different stories for each of us. Let us not be tempted to believe You are not working for us just because someone else's story seems to be unfolding first. Lord, we believe that just as You say in Romans 8:28, You are indeed working all things out for Your glory and our benefit. We praise You, oh Lord. Let us trust the path, even when it looks bleak. In Jesus' name, Amen.

WHEN THE UGLY DUCKLING GREW UP

Do you recall the story of the ugly duckling from long-ago nursery stories? In short, there was an ugly duckling that was mocked when she wasn't ignored, and no one really got to know her true character. She then grew up into a beautiful swan, and the story ends. Unfortunately, the story never shares how the ugly duckling didn't actually change inside, even if her exterior looked different.

When I was in middle school, there was a little game centered around hurting nerds. Like me. It involved boys daring other boys to ask out people like a teacher, janitor, maintenance worker, or me. High school was a free-for-all with kids mocking my clothes, my interests, and the fact that I got good grades in school. The only time I did get attention was when they needed someone to copy homework from or tutor them for a big test. Mind you in all of this, I am in no way complaining or playing a tiny little violin. I was a chubby middle schooler who grew into an anorexic high schooler wearing clothes from the clearance rack and wide-rimmed glasses a decade before they were all the rage. Braces, an introverted and shy demeanor, and issues at home didn't help much either. But I was me, through and through. I spent my Friday nights reading books on England's royal dynasties, meddling with the guitar, and writing poetry. For the most part, I was relatively happy. The sad part was I didn't allow myself to be truly authentic; I felt something was wrong with me and I began to hate who I was. Not knowing how to "fix" myself, I was honestly really cruel to myself—starving myself endlessly and becoming a total bag of bones.

Senior year came to a close with a full scholarship, contacts, no braces, and clothing from Aeropostale. My friend Leah taught me how to apply makeup and, for the first time, I was becoming that swan. Ironically, the most popular boy in school complimented me...on the last day of school. The years that followed were nothing short of confusing for me. I thought any invitation out was a cruel joke, and even more alarming I found that the same kind of girls who once mocked me for how I looked now hated me for being pretty.

I was still the history-loving nerd within, even if my face changed. That is where the Ugly Duckling tale fails—it never tells what happened afterward. Years passed and truly by the grace of God I found my worth in Him. I found my identity in Him, and I found myself in Him. No longer is my worth or happiness tied up in the opinions of others, but in His opinion of me. But I would be lying if I said I still don't stand baffled when I get stares and not glares. I would be lying if I said I know how to handle attention. But I'm thankful for who I am, and moreover whose I am.

I'm not so arrogant to think that I am a remarkable beauty, but I do realize I am not the same lonely nerd of high school. I'm just the lonely adult nerd who teaches kids history. Honestly, that is what helped shape me to want to teach. When I worked for the Apple Store I helped facilitate a few field trips, and one of those was with a group of twelve-year-old girls. One little girl reminded me a lot of myself, so timid and sweet. The other girls were making fun of her for bringing a Barbie doll on the field trip. Suddenly I realized that although the girls were different, this was all still the same as when I was twelve.

So, I did something about it. I chimed in about how I had a similar doll when I was their age, and how cool it was. The "cool" girls thinking I was cool (ha!) quickly changed their tune and complimented the girl instead. That situation changed me. I realized the role a teacher can play in situations such as these, and I wanted to do that. Many other things influenced my decision to teach, of course, but this monumental day showed me that we adults have a wonderful duty to change the future. We can stop the cycles of bullying and unjust ridicule by our influence. It won't snuff out the fires of every bully, but it can make a difference.

With that, that's the point. No one has gone through life without a moment of bullying or hurt, whether you were the victim or the victimizer, but we can change the future. We can choose love over hate, and we can teach it to the next generation. We can raise up a generation that focuses on what we have in common over what sets us apart. We can encourage kindness over being rude. And we can love. Be the change you want to see in the world, y'all.

Prayer

Dear Lord,
We praise You for working in our lives. We praise You that even
when our lives look as if we are perpetually fixed in one place,
You are working in the background. Lord, we praise You for
this, and we pray that we would not be resistant to Your inner
workings in us. We praise You, oh God.
In Jesus' name,
Amen.

EATING DISORDERS

Since the fall of man, the concept of shame has plagued humankind. In the account in Genesis, we read that after Adam and Eve ate the forbidden fruit and sinned for the first time, they hid themselves. In shame over what they had done, they found coverings to cover their nakedness. They created a separation between them and God, and it terrified them. Thousands of years later, are their offspring really all that different?

Shame will manifest itself in many different ways and its root can come from various places. Perhaps it is a complex of not feeling loved, or being poorly loved, or not feeling adequate or good enough. Perhaps it is something hidden very deep in the crevasses of the soul that we would rather not have brought up. But shame will make people do things to themselves that they wouldn't do to their worst enemy.

For some, this self-hatred and shame will manifest in an eating disorder, like it did with me. In my blogs I've gone into my eating disorder at a pretty minimal level. I felt so proud that up to a few months ago I was four years clean. I went four years silencing those loud voices in my head encouraging me to hurt myself, to hate myself. But then I relapsed.

James 5:16 encourages us to confess to one another, and I suppose this is my confession. Not only did I relapse into my anorexic tendencies again, but I became bulimic: I made myself vomit on purpose. I say this very seriously, for what I did was so wrong. I took this body, this beautiful body given to me by God Himself, crafted so finely to be an image bearer for Him on earth, and I treated it like trash. I shamed it for any ounce of fat, called it ugly and less than, and deprived it of food like a prisoner. But isn't that what the enemy wants? For us to be prisoners of his in the mind, held captive by lies and deceit? And to make it worse, I made this body cough up food on purpose. The amount of shame I felt was overbearing. Not only this, but I stood in front of eighth-grade girls in a small group I lead and encouraged them that week in their own beauty and adequacy, yet I made the body I abide in feel the exact opposite. Jesus calls us to love others as ourselves, but perhaps at times we also need to love ourselves like we love others.

The main difference with this relapse was that I fully left this shame and pain at the foot of the cross. I didn't merely take it to God while still holding it in my hand, but I left it right there in its full ugliness and gave it to Him. I stopped hiding it from Him like Adam and Eve did; I let Him see it. The response was honestly the most beautiful occurrence and revealed to me more of the character of God. I felt loved. In all the shame I felt, in the condemnation I felt I deserved, He just loved me.

As I write this portion of the book, it is Good Friday. I am reminded of another sinner who felt he deserved shame and punishment for his behavior, but instead was blown away in surprise. As the thief on the cross hung next to Jesus on Calvary, in courage he left his shame literally at the cross, and what he found was love. Jesus told him that he would be in paradise with Him that very day. This is the story of Christ—He takes the shame we should carry for the sins we commit, and He washes us clean with His blood. In return, He gives us love.

I encourage you, whatever your shame, to give it to Him. Whatever holds you prisoner, whatever could make you freeze in terror if anyone ever knew, just give it to Him. Give Him your shame, and let Him give you love in return. It is not deserved, but that is the very definition of grace. God didn't make us so that we would have to (or could ever) earn anything to deserve it. For He is a Good Father, and He gives good gifts solely because of that. Let go of the shame; hand it to Him. He will bring beauty from those ashes, and the label that once was a scarlet letter on your chest will become the very thing you can testify that He set you free from and loved you through.

Prayer

Dear Lord,
Thank You for healing. Thank You that You see us
just as You saw the first man and woman made
in Your own image. Help us not to fall prey to the traps
set by the enemy that we are less than or not beautiful.
Help us to see ourselves and others as You do.
Lord, we praise You that You are a God who
makes beautiful things, and we pray that we would
not only believe that, but live that out.
In Jesus' name,
Amen.

FORGIVENESS

We've all heard the saying, "Holding a grudge is like drinking poison and hoping the other person dies," but it holds a lot of truth. Not a single person on the planet can say they've never been wronged or hurt and needed to forgive someone. Yet the truth of the matter is, forgiveness is extremely hard to do at times. It is only natural to want to hold on to that bitterness, to cling to that chip on our shoulders complaining that we were wronged, but what if we instead shoved those chips off our shoulders and walked free? What if we actually realized that we aren't perfect or blameless either? What if we took to heart all that we have been forgiven of?

Ephesians 4:32 remarks, "Be kind and compassionate to one another, forgiving each other, just as in Christ God forgave you." God sent His own Son to take our punishment on the cross and forgive our sins. Relient K says it best: "The beauty of grace is that it makes life not fair."[5] We don't deserve grace or goodness or blessings, yet Christ died for us still. We lie, cheat, steal, hurt others, idolize the wrong things, yet He forgave us. You may have read that list and felt exempt from committing those sins, but I bet you dollars to donuts that if you really think about it, you're guilty of committing one of those even today. This chapter isn't to make you feel guilty, but rather to help you rejoice that you are forgiven when you take your sins to the cross. Being given that freedom, that gift of our debt being fully paid, how can we not share that? How can we not forgive others as God forgave us?

Forgiveness truly is a choice, and a hard one at that. For a long time, I held on to the hurt imposed on me by someone I cared very much for. He let me go around and around in my head about my own flaws, imperfections, and issues because he was silent for so long. I wrote him nasty letters laying so much guilt on him (then I stashed them under a bed), but it was in a tearful moment of prayer that I realized the truth: he too is a flawed human. I am sure he would never consciously want to hurt me, but even if he did, he is human. He has his flaws, just as I do, and we will hurt each other whether we intend to or not. We will let our flesh win out over our spirits at times, and the results will sting those we care deeply about. But just as we would hope they would forgive us, we need to forgive others.

I hope I am not sounding preachy here, but it's vital to recognize the need for forgiveness. It is vital to act upon forgiving.

There is also the aspect of forgiving yourself for things. That can almost be harder, for you have to allow yourself to be free from the guilt of something you've caused or done. That weight is heavy and burdensome, at times overwhelming. Truly, taking the need to forgive yourself or others to Christ is the only way to be truly free. He can, and He will, help you move forward. You just have to ask.

Prayer

Dear Lord,
We thank You for forgiveness. We thank You
that You died so that we may live, and that You did this
not because we deserve it by our works, but because
You are a God of Love. Lord, we pray that just as You
forgave us, we would be able to forgive those who
have wronged us, and even forgive ourselves.
As You say in Your prayer, "Forgive us our sins,
for we also forgive everyone who sins against us."
Lord, help us in this journey. Help us beyond our own
fleshly desires to hold grudges and help us to walk into
the freedom that comes from truly forgiving.
In Jesus' name,
Amen.

WHAT SUCCESS LOOKS LIKE

What is success? How do we accurately measure something that is so arbitrary, for success is really a measure of opinion more often than not. If success, like beauty, is in the eye of the beholder, how then do we truly say whether someone is successful or not? What does the Bible say of success?

Perhaps the best example of a measure of success is in the parable of the talents in Matthew 25. In the story, a master gives three servants either one, two, or five talents of money. The one with five invests his money and comes back with ten. Likewise, the one with two invests and comes back with a return as well. But the last one takes a different approach; in fear, the servant with a single talent buries his money. When standing before the master to give an account, the first two are honored with more responsibility, but the one who chose to bury his talent was condemned, for he wasted what he had been given. This is a good measure of success. To whom much is given, much is required (see Luke 12:48). Let that sink in again: to whom much is given, much is required. So, then, what is required of us?

Micah 6:8 says, "He has showed you, O man, what is good. And what does the LORD require of you? To act justly and to love mercy and to walk humbly with your God." We are all given unique skills sets, different gifts, and various challenges from day one of this life. What is important is how we put them to use for God's Kingdom. The key is to realize that talents are not always what we would think of when it comes to gifts. At times these talents can feel burdensome, but what if we used these hard knocks in life to become the foundation of our testimonies? What if we used the difficulties in life to propel us further in Christlikeness? What if even the hard aspects of life would make us better instead of bitter?

One of the most overlooked, but amazing, miracles was the healing of Bartimaeus (Mark 10). He was blind, and he came to Jesus for help. Many of the people Jesus had healed just turned and walked away—in essence, taking their "talents" and burying them. Bartimaeus instead followed Christ. He saw in Jesus the fulfillment of the promised Savior, and went on to share the gospel for the rest of his life. He began his life with very little, but he used what he was given to make him better and not bitter. He took his gift and produced an abundance of fruit.

Our time here on earth is short, so we should use every stitch of our time well. The Bible tells us that we should be "making the most of every opportunity, because the days are evil" (Ephesians 5:16). How tragic a life would be if it were squandered; how heartbreaking it would be if we were saved and didn't bother to share the good news with others!

Success in a worldly mindset typically involves wealth, fame, or looks. God shows us that true success is a fruitful and deep relationship with Him, doing the work He calls us to do here on earth. That doesn't mean that fame is bad. If anything, fame or position is a full five talents, to be used for His glory and ministry more than for our own selfish ambitions.

How can we put that into practice? For starters, we can be kind. We can have courage. We can stand for Christ even when it's hard. We can be kind to those whom the rest of the world shuns. This can be as simple as reaching out to the quiet person who looks lost in the crowd, or being kind to a homeless person on the street corner. It can mean boldly showing the world what it really means to be a follower of Christ. The world has been deceived with the lie that a follower of Christ is judgmental, hard, hurtful, and hateful, and it is our duty to prove them wrong. A day lived in kindness and sharing the love of Christ is a day well lived.

We can do everything in our power not to squander the time we are given. God is the only One who knows how many days we have left, so we should use each day to its fullest. Let us not grow weary in the work, and when we do, let us come to Him for comfort. Let us be assured that our work, even if we cannot see the fruit, is not in vain. Let us know that the Holy Spirit is alive and at work in each of our lives all the time. Let us hold firm to these truths and let us go forward believing them, for one day (if even in heaven) we will see the abundant harvest.

Dear Lord,
Thank You for the fact that success is not something measured by
wealth or education, but by working each day to glorify You. Let
us not grow weary that our effort is in vain if we do not see the

fruit harvested on this side of the veil; rather, let us hold firmly
to the knowledge that You see all and know all, and that all will
work for Your glory in the end. Use us, oh Lord; use us well so
that we may hear one day, "Well done, good and faithful servant!"
In Jesus' name,
Amen.

WAKE UP

More than anything, I desire this book to be something that any reader can relate to and absorb some of its pointers or lessons. This section is about something every woman of God must go through: waking up.

In April 2017, my cousin and I prayed for hours for something we deeply cared about. That afternoon I was exhausted and decided to take a nap. During this slumber, I had a dream that was, well, unique. In the dream, I saw myself sleep. Same washed olive-green Henley, same brown-and-white quilt, same pictures on the wall. As I watched myself sleeping, suddenly an older version of myself came walking in. She was fearless. An absolute fearless warrior, but instead of boastful pride she was clothed in dignity and white, with flowing waist-length hair. She did not look down, nor she did stumble as she strode in with self-assured confidence. She was poised, humble, and walked with pure love and kindness. Gently this woman knelt by my bedside, placed a hand on my back, then whispered something to me. And with that I woke up. For months, I wrestled with what all of that meant, but more than anything I desired to become her. She was a strong woman of God who had seen His faithfulness. I imagine a bit like Hannah, the mother of Samuel, after her hope was fulfilled.

God brought to mind Isaiah 51, and I feel it is pertinent for every woman seeking after Him. Isaiah 51:9–16 says,

Awake, awake! Clothe yourself with strength,
  O arm of the LORD ...
Was it not you who dried up the sea,
the waters of the great deep,
who made a road in the depths of the sea
so that the redeemed might cross over?
The ransomed of the LORD will return.
They will enter Zion with singing;
everlasting joy will crown their heads.
Gladness and joy will overtake them,
and sorrow and sighing will flee away.

"I, even I, am he who comforts you.
Who are you that you fear mortal men,
the sons of men, who are but grass,
that you forget the LORD your Maker,
who stretched out the heavens
and laid the foundations of the earth,
that you live in constant terror every day
because of the wrath of the oppressor,
who is bent on destruction?
For where is the wrath of the oppressor?
The cowering prisoners will soon be set free;
they will not die in their dungeon,
nor will they lack bread.
For I am the LORD your God,
who churns up the sea so that its waves roar—
the LORD Almighty is his name.
I have put my words in your mouth
and covered you with the shadow of my hand—
I who set the heavens in place,
who laid the foundations of the earth,
and who say to Zion, 'You are my people.'"

We need to wake up and see the truth here. When we allow Him to come into our lives, and we become His children, we are His. He protects His own. No longer should we sleep in our own delusions that we are unworthy, disliked, an outcast. We need to wake up into the beautiful reality beyond this world. We need to wake up into the loving arms of Him who died to save us and make us free. And we need to realize it is in the *becoming* of who we already *are destined to be* that worth, beauty, and acceptance of one's self truly emerges.

I love the imagery of verse 11 that gladness and joy will come, and we will enter into this abundance with singing. This is not to say that waking up into this woman will be easy. In fact, it will be painful and hard at times. Hosea 6:1 says,

"He has torn us to pieces
but he will heal us;
he has injured us
but he will bind up our wounds."

In many ways, this is what sanctification looks like. In order for a muscle to grow, its fibers must be torn so that it can heal back bigger and stronger. That's why we find ourselves sore after a long workout, and that's why during seasons of sanctification in full force, we find ourselves feeling torn. In the darkest days the greater glory we must be attuned to, and hold so firmly to, is that those tears will be healed and made right. Those tears will make us stronger and better. Perhaps it's no coincidence that the same word "tear" is used for something that is torn and broken as well as for the droplets that fall from our eyes out of gladness and pain. Both are connected and are a great metaphor of His goodness.

So, wake up. Allow those tears to form and drop in front of Him, and you will be restored by Him in the right ways. Wake up into life, and life abundantly. There is perseverance to be built, which in turn makes for character, which births hope. (See Romans 5:3–5.) The hope in Him. Wake up into hope, my friends.

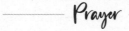 *Prayer*

Dear Lord,

Thank You that we can count on the sun to rise each morning, and in the same way, we can count on Your mercies. Lord, we pray that if we are not attuned to Your activity in our lives, You would "wake us up" to what You are doing. Just as Paul was blind and did not see until You opened his eyes, Lord, please open our eyes. Pour Your Spirit upon us and give us a new vision and glimpse into Your heart for us. Lord, we praise Your glorious name.

In Jesus' name,

Amen.

CHAPTER 3

Teammates

SEASONAL BLOOMS

"Bows before beaus." Yeah, I know that's not the phrase, but I am from the South and we don't say certain things in good company, so my Southern roots will now require me to offer a different phrasing. Nevertheless, it's Girl Code for putting your girl friends before guys. But what happens if the girls you are valuing that highly see a change in tide within your friendships?

Because all friendships involve relationships between fallen human beings, they too are flawed and imperfect. What is important to realize is that friendships can be given or adjusted by God for certain reasons and seasons.

Friendships are very dynamic and different from a relationship with a significant other or family member, because they do not carry a blood or vow commitment. They are mutually bound only by the weight of importance that both parties give the relationship, nothing more. This is why at different times you may find yourself closer to one friend and then even months later very distant from the person.

Friendships will go through various seasons in your life, because there will be times when you're both headed in different directions. There is nothing wrong with this, but it does not always feel comfortable.

Ecclesiastes 3:1 says, "There is a time for everything, and a season for every activity under heaven." The book of Ecclesiastes was written by Solomon, the wisest man to ever walk the earth, and what he said was very true. Everything has its season, including friendships. Some friendships are like flourishing olive trees that endure and sustain for a lifetime, but some are like cut flowers that last only a short while. The beauty is that God will bring the olive trees at just the right time, as He will the colorful blooms that make life a little grander for a while. What is key is letting Him have that say, and letting Him pull weeds when necessary.

Oftentimes we don't even realize weeds are growing until someone points them out to us or their true ugliness is eventually revealed. I spend a lot of time in my garden, and from time to time I will find a weed hiding in the midst of all the flowering strawberry plants, concealed so I nearly miss it until it grows large and creates a problem. That can be a metaphor for certain people in your life—you may not know they are a "weed" until they become a problem. More often than not, we miss seeing the weeds until they become an issue since we are on the same level as those strawberry plants. Everything looks green and healthy from eye level, but God can see from overhead. If every so often we let Him clean up our lives and clear out weeds, sure, we may lose friends, but we can also have more room to grow and more room for good and healthy relationships to come into our lives. Do not be afraid to pray out the weeds in your life; it may save you from a lot of heartache and issues in the long run.

At other times a friend may not be a weed, but God will still remove them from our lives, and it hurts. Even losing a friend by slowly drifting apart does not feel very comfortable. It's awkward and you find yourself wanting to text the person, but write and delete it five times before giving up. We feel saddened, confused, and lost at how to handle the loss of a friendship when there really wasn't a solid reason for it to end. The important key here is to trust God. That can never be said enough. God knows what is around the corner for you and for them, and it may not be the best season for your friendship to be as vibrant. It doesn't soften that pain as much as we would hope, but in time it usually becomes evident why those friendships saw a season of waning.

James 1:17 says, "Every good and perfect gift is from above, coming down from the Father of the heavenly lights, who does not change like shifting shadows." It's true that God does not change and that all good things come from Him. That being said, shouldn't we trust Him with all of our earthly relationships too? It's easier said than done, but ultimately, He is the giver of all good things, so when we place those relationships in His hands, He will give us His best for the season.

Here's another way to look at it. But sacrificing our own selfish wills and letting Him take the lead, we are offering to Him some of the most important and vital pieces of our lives. He sees that and cherishes it, not considering it to be worthless, and because of who He is, He blesses that offering. Malachi 3:10 says, "'Bring the whole tithe into the storehouse, that there may be food in my house. Test me in this,' says the LORD Almighty, 'and see if I will not throw open the floodgates of heaven and pour out so much blessing that you will not have room enough for it.'" In this case, we are offering these relationships, our time, and our will to Him. He promises that He will bless that, because, as it said in James, He is never changing or failing. God cares about all the little details in your life, and the company you keep will certainly have an impact on your life. He cares very much about that, and in trusting Him to direct every one of those relationships, He will direct you correctly.

Communication with friends is another very important aspect of a healthy friendship. If you find that a friendship is having issues or is waning, simply having a deep talk may change everything. That includes connecting with God to see if this friendship is something He has for you, or if it is not His will that you continue in relationship. As women, we feel such pressure to be perfect all the time, to hold our chins up and our feelings in, but much of the purpose of close girlfriends is that we can let all of that out. We can be comfortable and can share the inner parts of our lives. The importance is, being willing to be vulnerable within our friendships.

Let God be the Master Gardener of your life, and He will create fields of blooms for every season and reason under the Son. Be open to being vulnerable so you can be deeply rooted in those good friendships too. You never know what they might yield ahead.

Prayer

Dear Lord,
Thank You for the seasons. Thank You that each is wonderfully different, and thank You that we are able to experience that here on this earth. While we are on this side of the veil, it is often unknown what You have planned, but, Lord, we pray that we do not resist the changing seasons. We pray that just as the leaves do not refuse to change color in autumn, we would gracefully embrace Your changes and know that they are for greater vibrancy and glory and understanding in You.
In Jesus' name,
Amen.

BUILDING YOUR TEAM

Pack, gang, squad, or team—whatever you call them, you need people who have your back.

A wise person once said, "Show me your friends, and I'll show you who you are." There is such truth in that statement! The Bible has a similar saying: "Bad company corrupts good character" (1 Corinthians 15:33). Who you choose to surround yourself with affects how you act, what you do, what your life looks like. This is why it is actually a good thing to be picky about who you invest your time with.

Investing your time is a lot like investing your money: both are limited resources that can yield a good or bad return. Investing your time in people who build you up will result in good, whereas investing in people who tear you down and make you feel low will only lead to the demise of your self-esteem. Ecclesiastes 4:9,10 says, "Two are better than one, because they have a good return for their work. If one falls down, his friend can help him up." Though some apply this passage to spouses, it essentially means one person encouraging another person in Christ. There is no greater thing a friend can do than encourage someone in Christ. As you read this book, I sincerely hope you are at an upturn in your life where everything is working out well, but I can sadly promise that will not always be the case. When the world is falling apart around you, you will need a team of fellow believers to encourage you to fight the good fight, trust when there seems to be no way, and seek God in all things. A team is not merely a group of friends to enjoy life with, it's a group of friends to go through life with.

The concept of "going through life" can mean a friend, or group of friends, is woven into the fabric of your life—venturing through ups and downs, joys and sorrows, or just events and movie nights. This is what life is made up of: a million little moments connecting together into a dynamic and unique tapestry.

Going through life with friends often involves simple day-to-day events. It is taking a cycle class together a few times a week. It's phone calls on the drive home to spitball ideas on how to approach your boss about an issue. It is sitting in the waiting room as your close friends have their first child. It is all the little moments that add up to a life. And it is nothing short of beautiful.

Just like drafting for a good sports team, building your team takes patience, practice, and prayer. Pray for good and godly people to come into your life to help you grow as a person. God will usher in people into your life at just the right time. In Matthew 7:9–11, Jesus says, "Which of you, if his son asks for bread, will give him a stone? Or if he asks for a fish, will give him a snake? If you, then, though you are evil, know how to give good gifts to your children, how much more will your Father in heaven give good gifts to those who ask him!" So, ask!

Ask God to build your team, and with them build your life.

Dear Lord,
Thank You for friendships. Thank You for creating fellowships
with one another to grow and seek Your kingdom. Lord, You said
it is not good for man to be alone, and so, Lord, we pray that You
would build and foster "teams" of fellow believers with the goal
of glorifying Your name above all else. Help us to challenge each
other and build one another up, always keeping the focus on You.
In Your name,
Amen.

LOVE MANY, TRUST FEW

My grandmother had a little wooden sign in her house that read "Love many, trust few, and always paddle your own canoe." As Christians, we are called to indeed love all, but loving someone and trusting someone are two different things entirely. I think about even my closest friendships and how deep the wound has gone when they've broken my trust, but I also regret in hindsight how I have let those jaded feelings of protecting my heart raise up my walls too high. So, what is the right way to approach trust?

Trust is a lot like respect; it must be given and maintained but can be hard to earn back once broken. Forgiveness must be offered first before any trust is rebuilt. Angela Thomas said,

> When a woman has a kingdom heart, she has an active understanding of what matters most to the heart of God. She lives in the balance of passion and contentment. She learns to love well, give without regard to self, and forgive without hesitation.
>
> The woman with a kingdom heart may have a duffel bag full of possessions or enough treasures to fill a mansion, but she has learned to hold them with an open hand…
>
> Hold everything with open hands…I don't think we're ever allowed to grab hold of anything or anyone as though they matter more than the kingdom of heaven…
>
> When you hold relationships with open hands, then people come in and out of your life as gifts of grace to be cherished and enjoyed, not objects to be owned and manipulated…And then when you hold your dreams with open hands, you get to watch God resurrect what seemed dead and multiply what seemed small.[6]

There is so much in this quote that just grabs me, but I think a lot of the meat here is about open hands. If we allow these relationships where we build trust to first be rooted and established in love (in God), then whether He causes them to end or flourish, it is okay. We are okay, even if that friendship ends for a time or for good.

I think that is what trust really is rooted in—trust in God. Then trusting everyone else becomes secondary. By all means broken trust can hurt, but forgiveness can come about too. So, love many, trust few deeply, and paddle that canoe.

Dear Lord,
Trust is such a tricky thing to navigate. Help us know when to guard our hearts, or when to let down our walls and embrace people fully. Lord, You and You alone know the proper and correct methods of this with each individual circumstance, and, Lord, we pray for Your direction and love in this.
In Jesus' name,
Amen.

WHEN A FRIEND GETS A BOYFRIEND

Like the seasons, relationship dynamics change with time. This change is a part of life, and it is a part of getting older. This is especially true when a friend gets a boyfriend, or a spouse, or a child. Each of those new normals cause the friendship to change in some way; if it remains completely the same, a large portion of that person's life is being left out of your friendship with them. The question then comes up, what do you do when your friend gets a significant other and you are still single?

For starters, it is important to be supportive. It is an exciting event when a friend finds someone she clicks with, and it is important to let her know you support her. This is an opportunity for you to make a good friend as well in that new person, and more often than not, good people know good people. There is a good chance too that your friend will be a little insecure in a brand-new relationship and will look to you for support and love during this time. Let your friendship be a safe zone where your friend can speak freely and openly, trusting that all that is said will be held in confidence.

What about jealousy? It is a natural emotion to become jealous, especially if you feel like someone "stole" your best friend. But she will not seem to be occupied by the new person in her life forever; she will still need a best friend. Who else is going to go with her to get her nails done? Who else will be there for the conversations just gals can have? Who else will do that spin class with her? You are not being replaced; your relationship dynamics are just changing. One day you will have someone too and it will change again, so don't let jealousy on your end ruin your friendship.

What about red flags you see? I've always said, the way I can tell if a friend has found "the one" is that she is the very best version of herself I've ever seen. There have been times where I've seen massive red flags in the person a friend has chosen, such as a controlling manner, pulling her away from God, or having bad behaviors. In this case, be gentle. Be supportive of your friend, but do not always be silent. Kindly and gently present your concerns, but be very careful in how you approach it. Above all else, pray for that person and the entire situation. I've actually prayed that if the couple was not meant to be, God would break them up. Or if they were meant to be, that God would allow my view to change to better see the good in it all. God is in control, but we must let Him drive for events to take place in His timing.

When a boyfriend becomes a husband, it is a new ballgame then as well. Suddenly your friend is living with this guy of hers, and her time of course will be spent with the spouse more than on her own friends. Again, this is when it is important to be loving, gentle, and patient with your friend. Rejoice with the couple in this new season, that God has blessed a relationship as far as marriage; rejoice in the new freedoms and experiences they have to enjoy. One day the favor will be returned, and they will be rejoicing alongside you as well.

Prayer

Dear Lord,
Thank You for the gift of friendship. Thank You that our
friendships grow and change along with us. Help us to be mature
in our friendships, and above all else glorify You in them, so that
we may enjoy the kinds of beautiful friendships You destined for
us to have. Help us not to become jealous, anxious, or insecure;
rather, let us come into the abundance of what You have to give us
through the fruit of Your Spirit.
In Jesus' name,
Amen.

CHAPTER 4

Dating

TO QUOTE CHARLIE BROWN, "I GOT A ROCK"

Today in the mail was yet another wedding announcement, this time for the younger sibling of a friend. So not only are all my friends married off now, some even with children, but it seems their younger siblings are beating me to the sacred altar as well. It can be easy to become bitter. It can be easy to fall into the mentality that there is something wrong with you, or that you are infected with some sort of plague.

Singleness really has become the modern-day equivalent of leprosy, hasn't it? Your married friends avoid inviting you to things, so you won't "feel out of place at a couple's event" or well-meaning relatives ask if you've tried sites like Christian Mingle, which can yield results for some people. But what if it isn't that there is something wrong with you, rather that God is just not finished working on you yet? That you're holding out for the best person God has for you, and along the way He is developing you as well? What if it's not that we are being patient and waiting on

God, but that He's waiting on us to just let down our strongholds and trust Him?

The unfortunate downside of beautiful things is that they are rarely all that spectacular while they're being made or refined. How often do we look at a pile of dirt and find it lackluster while just below the surface the first shoots of a flower are ready to burst forth? The same can be said of us. Of us, of people, of the seasons of refinement when the work being accomplished in us feels anything but beautiful.

In Matthew 7:9–11, Jesus highlights that earthly fathers, as human as they are, wouldn't hand their son a stone if he asked for bread, or wouldn't give him a snake if he asked for fish. So, then, how much more will your heavenly Father give good gifts when you ask Him? When I read this passage, something about it struck a chord. I myself have felt stuck in a season of perpetual waiting. Not just mere waiting, but refinement and pruning (think a waiting room in hell where your name is never called, but rather you're set on fire daily and Taylor Swift is playing on repeat). Perhaps I am being a bit overdramatic, but at times it has felt like Hades.

During these times, in my Bible readings God would constantly take me to every place in the Bible where He said, "The stone the builders rejected has become the capstone." Of course, I knew the Bible was referring to Jesus, but how did that pertain to me? Last time I checked I wasn't in the construction business.

I recall wailing out to God one afternoon on my bed, sobbing over how lost and confused I felt. I had done every single thing He had called for, I strived to be so perfect, yet nothing seemed to change. Things just got worse. I begged for this bread, reminding Him of Matthew 7. Instead of the flood of manna I expected to fall from the sky, it was hailstorm after hailstorm. I felt pelted by rocks left and right. But it was this overabundance of rocks that laid the foundation for what would one day become a massive testimony in my life. It was the rocks I was given that I didn't want, the rocks I rejected of patience, courage, tears, and learning my own strength that would become the cornerstone of a testimony He was building. He built my life on this foundation.

He knew a bread foundation wouldn't last. It might be a piece of cake, but it would fall apart and soon be forgotten. The foundation of bread would grow stale and I would soon take it for granted.

However, a foundation of stone would last forever. The garden that would grow through these rocks would need deep roots that could only be indwelled by the richness of God Himself. This gift of stone instead of bread was just that: a gift.

We may not see it until it is finished or near completion, but one day the object offered to us and initially rejected by our human hearts may just be the very thing that defines us.

I'd like to think of myself as a formidable woman of God, a fortress standing strong against roaring waves as the Son shines down...but I am not. Oh, sure, I have my days, days where I dismiss fear and its shrill lies, but this past weekend was not one of those days. We seldom recognize that we live in a world at war. Not merely a war between people, but a war of good and evil unseen by human eyes. My understanding of this was not widely opened until high school when I read *The Screwtape Letters* by C. S. Lewis. Lewis vividly brings us behind the scenes of the underworld to view how Satan's minions push the little discrete buttons in every one of us to knock us down. For me, anxiety and depression are enduring thorns in my side that are at times pushed in hard enough to make me bleed. Paul describes the thorn that he endured:

> I must go on boasting. Although there is nothing to be gained, I will go on to visions and revelations from the Lord.

I know a man in Christ who fourteen years ago was caught up to the third heaven. Whether it was in the body or out of the body I do not know—God knows. And I know that this man—whether in the body or apart from the body I do not know, but God knows—was caught up to paradise. He heard inexpressible things, things that man is not permitted to tell. I will boast about a man like that, but I will not boast about myself, except about my weaknesses. Even if I should choose to boast, I would not be a fool, because I would be speaking the truth. But I refrain, so no one will think more of me than is warranted by what I do or say.

To keep me from becoming conceited because of these surpassingly great revelations, there was given me a thorn in my flesh, a messenger of Satan, to torment me. Three times I pleaded with the Lord to take it away from me. But he said to me, "My grace is sufficient for you, for my power is made perfect in weakness." Therefore I will boast all the more gladly about my weaknesses, so that Christ's power may rest on me. That is why, for Christ's sake, I delight in weaknesses, in insults, in hardships, in persecutions, in difficulties. For when I am weak, then I am strong. (2 Corinthians 12:1–10)

Paul was a mighty man of Christ, gifted with glimpses of the future, of Heaven, of things that can only be given by God. Though we think of the Bible as being written two thousand years ago, we must realize that the men and women in the Bible were exactly like us—ordinary humans. Like many of us, they were called to a greater purpose than the mundane lives we often aspire to and into a life of service for God. This service will yield no greater joy than Christ Himself, and no greater opposition than the enemy of God in every act.

I have been through such seasons of "boot camp" of sanctification and growth in the Lord, and I confess that I sometimes become a tad prideful in how far I've come in this journey and neglect to recall the most vital thing of all: I am not enough, and God is. Over a weekend I came to the end of myself, the end of my own strength, the end of my own understanding and controls, and I cried out to Jesus begging Him to come and surround me in His grace. I begged to hear His voice or to be given a comforting verse in His Word. In my time of need, He surrounded me with His love and made up for my lack by providing immeasurably more than all I could ask or imagine (see Ephesians 3:20). I do not believe God causes the thorns in our lives, but I do believe He allows them to endure at times so we can see our desperate need for Him.

At the end of ourselves we find a void, and the only thing that can fill that void is Christ Himself.

Prayer

Dear Lord,
Thank You that we know that even when it does not
make sense, You are working to grow us and fill us with
Your Spirit. We praise and extol You, oh Lord.
In Jesus' name,
Amen.

THE DESIRE TO HAVE A BOYFRIEND

One of the most memorable traits of high school is who is dating whom. It is an inescapable fact of life that during early high school the little alarms within our bodies seem to ring loudly, blaring, and in direct sight someone you paid no mind to the day before suddenly becomes surrounded by a choir of angels when he smiles.

More often than not, high school relationships start and end as fast as interest in a second-period science class.

There are instances where high school relationships actually pan out and become something more. One couple began dating in the tenth grade. It was the spectacle of the year when they broke up at the science fair, but they later ended up back together. They dated all through college and got married the week after graduation.

The key to remember, though, is that most high school relationships do not actually result in marriage. Out of everyone in my high school, the girl I most respected was named Maddie. Maddie had a rule for herself that she would not date until college. This was not because she wasn't sought after, popular, or desired, but rather because she had the wisdom to know she needed to mature into her own self before trying to form a relationship with someone else. The real question boils down to this: how can you share a relationship with someone else if you don't really know who you are?

It can be said that we spend our entire lives finding out who we truly are—and it is true that our lives are a journey into becoming who we truly are—but it is pertinent to have an understanding of your own personal goals, desires, and hopes before joining forces with another. More often than not, those aspirations will be what brings a couple together. This is often evident with ministry; countless couples will have the same calling from God for a place or a cause leading to a partnership built on God and commonality.

In truth, the sole way to find your identity is to find it in Christ. C. S. Lewis eloquently stated,

> Your real, new self (which is Christ's and also yours, and yours just because it is His) will not come as long as you are looking for it. It will come when you are looking at Him.

Does that sound strange? The same principle holds, you know, for more everyday matters. Even in social life, you will never make a good impression on other people until you stop thinking about what sort of impression you are making. Even in literature and art, no man who bothers about originality will ever be original: whereas if you simply try to tell the truth (without caring two pence how often it has been told before) you will, nine times out of ten, become original without ever having noticed it. The principle runs through all life from top to bottom. Give up your self, and you will find your real self. Lose your life and you will save it. Submit to death, death of your ambitions and favorite wishes every day and death of your whole body in the end: submit with every fiber of your being, and you will find eternal life. Keep back nothing. Nothing that you have not given away will ever be really yours. Nothing in you that has not died will ever be raised from the dead. Look for yourself, and you will find in the long run only hatred, loneliness, despair, rage, ruin, and decay. But look for Christ and you will find Him, and with Him everything else thrown in.[7]

What truth is found in this! In seeking Him, we find not only Him, but our true selves.

Think about it this way: when you purchase an appliance, do you just try to figure out by yourself how to run it, or do you check the manufacturer's instructions on how it works best? When it runs for years but then has an issue, what do you do? Will the problem be best solved by trying to fix it yourself, or by going to the maker to ask how to fix the issues with it? Trying it yourself will more than likely result in being covered in muck, frustrated, and more confused than ever. Your Maker knows how you are wired. He knows you so much better than you know yourself, and when you seek His help, He will know what is best.

Truett Cathy, founder of Chick-fil-A, often taught that life boils down to the "three M's": your Master, your mate, and your mission. What he was getting at is in the span of our lifetimes those three entities are what matter most in life. What is imperative here is making the choice to have the best of each of those. That comes through following Christ as your Master, and allowing Him to work in your life in the choice of marriage partner and in your life's mission.

The journey to finding yourself will lead you to God, and you may even go in with an entire slew of desires and aspirations all to find that in the end, He knows better. Trust the Maker, trust the journey, and trust the results will be worthwhile.

Prayer

Dear Lord,
We praise Your holy name. Lord, let us recognize that You are
the giver of all good things, and that every good and perfect gift
is from above. Let us be women of open palms, ready to hold or
release whatever You determine, without pushback. Lord, satisfy
our hearts in You, and prepare us for what You have planned
ahead.
In Jesus' name,
Amen.

THE FIRST DATE

Goodness, first dates are exhilarating and produce some of the bubbles of life. Everything is so new. Metaphorically you are standing at the threshold of a new door about to walk in and experience something you have not known before. Now, of course some first dates are going to be total duds—the kind you regret and wish you had spent time at home watching reruns of

The Office instead. Then some first dates are, well, the kind that leave you humming after you get home with rosy cheeks and that smile where you bite your lower lip just a little and swear the colors are just a little more vibrant than they were before. But let us not get ahead of ourselves here.

After saying yes to this potential date, you've spent an hour on your hair and the majority of the day thinking through what you have in your closet and whether you really need that new pair of heels. Now you're ready to go. You nervously wring your hands, as everything seems to be happening in such slow motion. You question back and forth about which topics you should bring up and what you should hold back.

Here are a few tips that I've learned over the years:

1. Be yourself. You aren't a "dime a dozen" girl, and it's important to show that you are unique. You aren't like the other fish in the sea—you are a mermaid.
2. Try to avoid topics such as politics or controversial ideas that could stir more of a debate, as debating isn't a great way to start a relationship.
3. If you have a good sense of humor, let that show.
4. Don't wear clothes that are too revealing. Find something fitted enough to show you've a woman, but loose enough that you're a lady. Wear what you feel confident in especially.
5. If you have a nerdy side, guys love that. An interest in *Star Wars*, *Lord of the Rings*, or video games is usually a good thing to show off.
6. Always have breath mint and lipstick ready for a refresh.
7. Be genuine and real; don't act fake or tell a single lie. Be honest and true to yourself and to God above all else.
8. If you feel uncomfortable, don't suffer through the date or feel obligated to give a second one.

9. Ask your date about himself. Guys love talking about themselves and you'll learn more about them that way too.

10. Don't order anything to eat that's messy, like ribs or pasta.

11. Listen more than you speak, and observe more than you convey.

12. Playing with your hair makes guys crazy; I have no idea why, but it just does. Twirling it or gently flipping it will drive them mad, so avoid it.

13. The majority of guys do enjoy talking about cars, the outdoors, or sports so if you happen to enjoy any of those things too, don't shy away from showing your interests.

14. Don't kiss on the first date. Cheek kisses are all right, but hold off on the big first kiss until you know each other better.

Prayer

Dear Lord,
We give to You our dating lives. We know that dating is for the
intention of marriage, and we leave it in Your hands not to be
manipulated or misused. Please help us to be guided by your Holy
Spirit and not the spirit of our culture, so that everything
we do is pleasing to You.
In Jesus' name,
Amen.

IT'S NOT IN VAIN

I'll be honest: at times being single feels like some sort of punishment. If you're like me, you will see all your friends get married and start families before you ever have your first kiss. But I promise you this: it is not in vain unless you make it in vain.

The years between ages eighteen and thirty-five can be your most selfish. You have the most freedom in career, relationships, and life. You are typically looking your best during those years, and more than likely have the most opportunity to chase your own desires, dreams, and ambitions. But what if instead of living those years for yourself, you gave them to God?

In a society where "the world is your oyster," we give few pearls to Christ. I am not saying you should go check into the nearest nunnery for these years, but what if you really handed them over to God? What if we let Him take the driver's seat, and we just trusted that He will take us to a place where we are truly happy? Oh, and along the way, we get to know the Driver all the better.

We think we know exactly what we want, how we should go about it, and what is best. The truth is, we don't. The truth is that what God will lead us through may not seem kind or good, but it defines who we are more often than not. In nearly every instance, we are given the choice to become cold and hardhearted, or to embrace it as something that helps us grow and changes us for the better.

During these years many of you will be single. Many of you will have to choose between taking the guy you know with no shadow of doubt is danger and a bad idea, and telling him no and waiting for the one who is God's choice for you. You will have opportunities to make choices that lead to consequences, whether good or bad. You may also have times where you ask God which way to go, and He is silent. That is when you have to trust your instincts. Trust what you know of God. Trust what you have read in Scripture. Trust that He is there. Remember that God does truly care.

I used to look bitterly toward God because He kept me single so long. I used to hold so much contempt toward God for how many years I was having to wait for my mate. I cried countless tears and begged and bargained and looked up to see nothing. Then God changed my perspective. I asked God to open my eyes after reading a story in 2 Kings 6 about Elisha's servant, who saw only the problem; but when God opened his eyes, he saw the solution: that God had it all covered. God helped me to realize that in these past few years He has grown my relationship with Him to be something so much stronger and enduring than I could have ever imagined. He has helped me to grow in maturity and in myself, so that without a shadow of doubt I truly know who I am. God helped me learn to receive love, and to overcome all the pitfalls I had within myself not knowing how to love or be loved. He helped me write books and start jobs and walk forward toward my calling. Sure, I dated some frogs that never became princes but He used that too. He used my mistakes to be markers of His grace. One of my favorite quotes is from Lisa Bevere: "If you think you've blown God's plan for your life, rest in this: you, my beautiful friend, are not that powerful." He uses the bad for good too.

We offer a sacrifice to God to take this time and hand it over to Him. It is a sacrifice to deny ourselves worldly desires and to trust and follow Him, even when it does not make sense. But God sees those sacrifices; He sees when we choose Him over our flesh. He does not turn a blind eye or shrug it off—it matters. I truly believe those sacrifices come back to us as blessings. Though we have to suffer the consequences of poor choices, we grow a deeper trust in Him to give us better than what the world has to offer. We come to a greater knowledge of who He is and who we are in Him. We come to see that this world and this time are all so fleeting. Suddenly the old and melancholic King Solomon does not sound so morbidly depressing in Ecclesiastes, but rather wise. For he knew that God was worth more than anything this world can offer. God does not scoff at our sacrifices, nor does He turn away anyone earnestly seeking His face.

When it comes to relationships, we can seek them on our own, or we can look to our Creator. In my humble opinion, it is always best to let Him direct everything. He made you, so He is the only one who knows truly who is the best fit for you. He knows who your best teammate is, He knows who He thought of when He made you, and likewise you were in His thoughts as He created your future mate. In Genesis 2:18 God tells us that it is not good for man to be alone, and Ecclesiastes 4:9–12 says two are better than one and a cord made of three (God, you, and your husband) is not easily broken. Why would you ever want to settle for anyone less than who God specifically crafted for you?

This is my challenge to you: Ask. Seek. Knock. (See Luke 11:9.)

Ask God to direct your heart daily. Keep your eyes so completely focused on Him that only through His lenses could you ever see the one He made for you. Pray against temptations. Seek God's will over your own, praying for every crush you have that if it is God's will, it will remain, but if not, it will be snatched quicker than you can begin to start doodling his name. Pray constantly for yourself and for your future spouse. You cannot pray for someone too much.

Sacrifice those years to God as an offering. Let Him direct your path, and I promise He has a plan and He will not fail. Even if it looks dark right now, keep walking in the Light. It will be worth it in the end.

Prayer

Dear Lord,
Let us keep in mind that our efforts are not in vain. Help us hold
firm to the knowledge that You are indeed ever working in our
hearts to purify and grow us into the women that You destined us
to be. Let our hearts be flesh and not stone, and able to be molded
to Your liking and for Your glory.
In Jesus' name,
Amen.

A DANGEROUS PRAYER ABOUT BOYS

Especially when you are younger, it is so easy to fall into the mindset of "be young and free," but that freedom comes at a cost. This is not to say that marriage should be the central focus when it comes to every fleeting crush or blushing encounter, but it is vital to allow God to hold your precious heart. Your heart is the most precious gift you can offer to another, and placed in the wrong hands it can be severely broken or manipulated. It is such a human condition, and really the root of the first sin, to think that somehow we know better than the Creator Himself, but the fact is we do not. Isaiah 44:2 shares, "This is what the LORD says—he who made you, who formed you in the womb, and who will help you: Do not be afraid, O Jacob, my servant, Jeshurun, whom I have chosen."

Before we were even born God saw every single aspect of our lives, and therefore it would be completely ignorant to think that we in any way know better than Him. Yet in our own flesh and rebellion more often than not we live like we do somehow know better. The beauty of the truth of Christ is that no matter how deep a mess we find ourselves in, He is still there to help pick us back up. We can certainly save a lot of mess and tears in trusting His hand to guide us.

Where does this leave us when it comes to guys? What are we to ask for or do? There are many different ways to pray when it comes to dating, but truly one of the best prayers you could ever pray is to ask God to change your heart if the particular guy, or even dating in that season, is not for you. Jeremiah 6:16 shares what the LORD says: "Stand at the crossroads and look; ask for the ancient paths, ask where the good way is, and walk in it, and you will find rest for your souls." Psalm 34:10 assures us that "those who seek the LORD lack no good thing." What these verses are compelling the listener to do is to ask God. If this brave praying woman finds herself beginning to have feelings for a guy, she will take it to God first. She would sacrifice her own headstrong feelings and in sincerity ask God to guide her feelings. If the feelings were to persist, she would know it was of Him, but if they dissipated, that was of Him as well. I cannot tell you how, time after time, those I know who have prayed this simple surrendering prayer have been spared from some major heartbreaks.

That leads us to the concept of sacrificing for the Lord. What is sacrifice? Sacrifice is placing something precious upon the altar of God for His use. In ancient times this typically meant a lamb or dove, but we no longer live in times where that is necessary, for through Christ's sacrifice on the cross our sin debt is paid and the curtains are torn between God and us. Today we too can sacrifice to Him, but with our hearts. We can place our hearts on the throne of God most holy, offer Him the most sacred and unique possession we can obtain, and trust Him radically to give us His best. This may bring us to a time of loneliness, or this may lead us to a time of hard-core sanctification, but it is worth it completely. For God knows us so intimately that He knows what is helpful and what is harmful to our very souls. Trusting Him with such a relationship will only lead to the ultimate best choice for your love life.

Recognize that in those times of waiting, sacrificing, and letting Him lead, we grow in our trust as well. Patience is not about *time*, it is really about *trust*. We can trust that He is good, and that in fact this journey ahead will turn out for good. Having patience in any circumstance is not meant to be a prison sentence, for in that we confuse *patience* with *consequence*. Consequences come from choices we make and the aftermath may require cleanup or repair. Consequences can take time as well, but for mending. Patience on the other hand is about trust. Trusting that the current time holds purpose, and that it is more about our journey and growth than it is the passage of time. This is where patience becomes less about waiting and more about action in the present.

Prayer

Dear Lord,
Thank You for the great reminder that we should place all things
before Your throne for proper placement. Let us not cling so tightly
to what we see easily accessible, but let us submit our hearts to You
and delight ourselves in You as Psalm 37:4 says, knowing that
only then will You mold us to give us the desire of our hearts. Let
our greatest desire always be You, in sincerity.
In Jesus' name,
Amen.

WHAT IS TOO FAR?

In a world where it seems everything goes, where do we draw the boundary lines? How far is too far when the world says "all the way" is A-okay?

If we are to dive into the Scriptures about this subject, we have no better resource than the Song of Solomon. Song of Solomon is a book in the Bible written by King Solomon himself about his dating and marriage to his wife. The entire book is centered around God, a man, and a woman, and the journey from dating to marriage. It's of utmost value, for it is the only book that is completely on the subject of marriage and sex, and it's something we can draw upon when we are questioning what is right and wrong physically.

It's important to know that sex is not sinful…inside marriage. Sex was designed by God for a husband and a wife to enjoy; it actually is the second command God gives mankind. After telling Adam not to eat from the tree of knowledge of good and evil, God then tells the happy couple to be fruitful and multiply (as Nike would say, *just do it*). God even designed both the male and female bodies to not just perform sex to make children, but to have pleasure from the act. What cannot be stressed enough is that sex is *only for marriage*.

Song of Solomon puts it this way: "Promise me, O women of Jerusalem, by the gazelles and wild deer, not to awaken love until the time is right" (Song of Solomon 2:7, NLT). God is imploring us to not "awaken" love until the time is right—in the context of marriage. Countless opinions outside of the Bible will suggest that "being in love" is good enough, but it is not. That covenant commitment of marriage is holy. The word "holy" literally means "set apart, sacred," and sex is a holy act. Sex should be viewed as such, as something so beautiful and holy that it is very much worth the wait.

As Elisabeth Elliot explains, "The bicycle given for Christmas will not be prized like the bicycle bought with the money earned by delivering newspapers for two or three years." What she is getting at is that the desired object will produce more satisfaction when there is more anticipation, more hype, more excitement because you waited. Just like waiting until Christmas morning for presents, it will be a million times better.

Another opinion of the world is that everything-but-sex is all right, but that is not the case either. Though I am a very discreet person, I feel it necessary to dive in on such matters—because they do matter. The Bible does not give complete guidelines for all the aspects of being physical, but it does hint at quite a few.

Kissing can be fine and dandy. The key to remember here is that kissing can awaken desire and quickly become out of hand. There's a big difference between a respectful kiss goodnight and making out, which can lead to hands where they shouldn't be. Solomon does not address this, but in the sense of not "awakening love" it is best not to rev the engines while in park.

Outside of marriage, oral sex is definitely not okay. People have different opinions on the subject even within marriage, but John Piper speaks on it well: "Oral sex is even more intimate and delicate, it seems, than copulation. And we know this because even married couples are wondering if they should go there. It is as if it is a stage of intimacy that may not even be proper for married people. And to think it can be an innocent substitute for copulation, so people can obey the letter of the law outside marriage, is a mirage."[8] He goes on to say that, within marriage, it is right only if both parties feel it is kind and comfortable. Here I just want to set the record straight that oral sex is not okay outside of marriage. It isn't some loophole on the virgin scale; it is way too far.

Boundaries are something that you must set on your own. Some people may feel comfortable only holding hands and may not want to cross any lines before marriage—and that is perfectly fine. If you think about it this way, if you truly love the person, you will wait. In addition, the amount of time you will be married will be so much longer than this time of dating and engagement; you will have total freedom then, so enjoy this time right now. Thoroughly enjoy the anticipation and the excitement, just as you enjoy Christmas Eve before the big Christmas morning.

Believe it or not, I am nearly twenty-nine years old and have never been intimate. I've had the opportunity quite a few times, but I've set a firm boundary, and I want this experience to be only with my husband. I didn't want to just waste it to get it over with, but rather save it to be a wonderful present. I want that to be something wonderfully precious I can give. In my marriage, I want to give all of me, and I just truly feel it would be beautiful to give my husband such a precious gift.

For many people, the boundary line is set a different point. In 1 Corinthians 10:23, Paul shares that although something is permissible, it does not mean it is beneficial. When it comes to physical relationships, this is very much the case. For example, one of my closest friends is waiting until her engagement to kiss. She and her boyfriend came to the shared conclusion through prayer and mature self-awareness that even kissing can lead down a road quickly. They also wanted to place an extremely high importance on coming to know each other deeply without adding a physical relationship into the mix to throw anything off. They felt this was the most appropriate boundary line for their relationship, and I have no doubt that the Lord will bless them abundantly for this mature step.

Now, if you are reading this and waiting is something you did not do, I don't want for one single millisecond for you to feel some sort of shame or condemnation. Conviction, on the other hand, is different, for it encourages us to act differently moving forward. In truth, not one of us is above sin. In fact, when a crowd wanted to stone a woman who had sex outside of marriage, Jesus stooped down and began writing in the sand, and many think He was writing the sins of those standing there holding stones in their hands. (See John 8:3–11.) What is key in this passage is that Jesus did not tell the woman what she was doing was peachy keen— far from it. He boldly conveyed to her to go and sin no more. Through Christ and only through Christ can we be forgiven and made clean and new again. So, in the case of sexual sin, let Him be your redemption, giving you a clean slate and a second chance. Though we can't undo the past, we can make different choices in the future. It is possible to be a given a redemption of purity through Christ, and it is more than possible to get it right moving forward. Let no man shame what Christ has forgiven in the truth of your self-worth and view of yourself.

It comes down to knowing your own weaknesses and owning them. You can ask God where to stop before the point of no return, and how to navigate not only in obedience to Him but in respect for one another. Truly, how much sweeter will it be on the other side of marriage knowing you honored Him and each other in this way.

Prayer

Dear Lord,
Thank You for the gracious gift of connecting with another
person. Thank You for the good and perfect gift indeed of physical
and emotional purity that can one day be given in complete love
to someone else. Lord, help us know the correct boundaries in
all things, and to trust Your leading and guiding hand with all
such things. Help us know that Your will for us is indeed worth
the wait, and that at the end there is so much glory for You and
immense blessings waiting for us and our future spouse.
In Jesus' name,
Amen.

CHAPTER 5

Frogs, Not Princes

SHOULD I DATE A NONBELIEVER?

One of the hardest questions single believers will face is whether or not they should date a nonbeliever. It is not an easily accepted answer, for, as with all relationships, the desires of the human heart weigh heavily on the decision.

The Bible actually addresses this very subject. In 2 Corinthians 6:14 Paul says,

> Don't team up with those who are unbelievers. How can righteousness be a partner with wickedness? How can light live with darkness? (NLT)

Though dating is not marriage, it is the precursor of marriage. In mature relationships, marriage rests on the back of the mind. Any dating relationship where the partners neglect to think about marriage really has very shallow intents, and in many ways is a waste of time for both parties. The concept of "teaming up" is important to recognize. Your future spouse should be your best teammate, but if your teammate isn't even playing the same sport as you, chances are your team will fall apart.

Not all unbelievers are bad people whatsoever, nor are they beyond finding a relationship with God, but that is not your job in dating them. So many people have convinced themselves that they're doing "missionary dating," where they hope that in dating a nonbeliever they will have an influence on that person and they will come to faith. Though this has seen success in some cases, it is far from the norm. Jesus did not call His followers to go and date the unsaved, but He did call them to befriend and minister to them. This can all be done outside of a romantic relationship and, if anything, adding romance to the equation would only take away from the intent to bring the person into a relationship with Christ.

A simple answer of "don't do it" does not take away the desire in the heart. But dating non-Christians can often be a tool of temptation leading believers to compromise their beliefs and go for what is available and easily accessible. We live in an instant-gratification world, and to have a tangible and easy relationship at hand can often be extremely hard to give up.

I found myself in this exact spot several years ago with a man I had come to have deep affection for. We had never dated but had been close friends for many years. Each time I thought something else would begin, it seemed an obstacle arose, and I eventually gave up and moved on, for it was not a relationship where God had planted the seed to endure. I was about to move across the country to Minnesota when I was asked to dinner by this close friend. I naively thought it was just dinner and not a date, but I was very wrong. He and I are both mature adults and in a season of life where marriage is more the intent of relationships than just summer crushes, and he implied his desire to marry. He mentioned what a good wife and mother I would be. I was sitting there with literally everything a girl wants to hear regarding how lovely, smart, kind, and wonderful she is and all, but the idea of a ring came with a horrendous catch. I knew he didn't love God, and I knew God didn't want this for me.

The bottom line is that someone who does not love God first and foremost cannot love you properly. God is love, so if a person does not know the highest form of love, they cannot know how to love truly and fully. C. S. Lewis said, "To love you as I should, I must worship God as Creator. When I have learnt to love God better than my earthly dearest, I shall love my earthly dearest better than I do now. In so far as I learn to love my earthly dearest at the expense of God and instead of God, I shall be moving towards the state in which I shall not love my earthly dearest at all. When first things are put first, second things are not suppressed but increased."[9]

What Lewis means is that in order to love to the highest expression of love, to love sacrificially and correctly, we must love others through Christ. If the person you are considering does not even believe in God, he does not know that love. You cannot share what you do not have, so lacking that most important aspect will only lead to heartache, disappointment, and downfall.

This is not to say that a Christian man will be perfect— after all, he is still human—but he will have that accountability backing him because of his relationship with God. He will know that as a husband he is called to love his wife as Christ loves the church (Ephesians 5:25), which means loving her even to the point of death.

The way my story ended was that I went back to my car and screamed at God. I sobbed all the way home and threw a little fit. Real mature, eh? But the fleshly parts of me had wanted to be with him so badly, it was a literal battle between my spirit and flesh. I prayed and as He is prone to doing, God answered in the Word. My Bible literally opened to 2 Corinthians 6:14 and I read the verse that contained my answer so clearly. It took time, prayer, and the Holy Spirit to help my flesh let go of what it wanted to cling to, for I did care for this person, but that did not justify my being with him. God is gracious, and I can attest firsthand that He will help us when we ask.

In choosing to not "team up" with a nonbeliever, we offer a sacrifice to God. What we sacrifice begins as the desires of the flesh and for the instant gratification that comes from having something right away, but what we gain is worth far more. What we gain is protection from a slippery slope of eventual frustration, heartache, and unfulfillment. What we gain is time that we didn't waste on our own follies. What we gain is looking to God to lead us in the right path for our lives. The man of your dreams may not come the day after you sacrifice the relationship with a nonbeliever, but God will be there. He will faithfully direct your path and make it straight, even when you don't understand what He's doing (Proverbs 3:5,6). God assures us that "those who hope in me will not be disappointed" (Isaiah 49:23), and He will bless you in the future.

What if you have already found yourself on the flipside of such a relationship and gotten very burned? There is hope for you too, just like there is hope for me. For God gives us perhaps the greatest promise of the Bible in Romans 8:28: "And we know that in all things God works for the good of those who love him, who have been called according to his purpose."

Take your situation to God and wait for an answer. He will give you the best route: "I am the LORD your God, who teaches you what is best for you, who directs you in the way you should go" (Isaiah 48:17).

God will not disappoint you, and He will bless you for trusting Him over your own flesh. It won't be easy, but in the end, it will be worth it.

Dear Lord,
Give us courage to believe that You will not disappoint and that
trusting in You is always in our very best interest. Give us courage
to hand over every relationship to You.
In Jesus' name,
Amen.

AN UNEXPECTED JOURNEY

It is a picture of grace that the story where you messed up becomes
the foundation of a later testimony. It's often a story in which
God takes the muck you made and shapes it into a beautiful vase.
For me, it involves a boy.

His name was Fitz. For the first few months, we were barely
acquaintances. He and I both attended a Young Adults group in
college, and he was just that skinny dude who played drums. Time
passed, and I ended up joining the Praise and Worship Team, and
that is where we really began to bond. We both had a true love
of music, and most of our favorite bands were the same as well.
It's a typical girl-meets-boy story for the most part, but in truth it
was so much more complicated than just that sort of label. In fact,
labels were what got us in trouble most; there wasn't one.

See, we were never really "official," but the truth was that
we were far more serious than most Facebook status couples.
Truthfully, we were more serious than most couples who end
up married. But that is the thing with an infatuation—you don't
realize you're entangled until you're in too deep and things
get real.

As the months passed, Fitz and I became closer and closer.
We played gigs together and of course had Worship Team so
we saw each other nearly every day. Even when we didn't, we

communicated constantly. Mornings were always greeted with a "good morning" text and nights usually ended around 2 a.m. falling asleep with the phone in my hand. I honestly do not know how I graduated with honors with the time I devoted to Fitz.

Part of me chooses to play the innocent victim card—that I was a tragically lonely girl starved for attention and desiring friends— and though some of that is accurate, it didn't make it right. Nor did it help that the one pursuing me was a tad overbearing too. But I let it persist for far too long.

The guilt weighed heavily upon me because I knew he wasn't who God had for me. That was clear through prayer and even what I saw of the fruit of our relationship, for there was no fruit. I had many sleepless nights of tossing and turning and begging God to somehow change the relationship, though the answer was as clear as Fitz's blue eyes. Yet I continued to choose momentary satisfaction. Isn't that the real root of sin—selfishness? The selfish desire to continue with something you know is not God's best, yet it satisfies a hole in your heart so you continue on.

It is interesting how memories work. The Polaroids in my head depict so many different occasions with the same feeling: slight satisfaction smothered in regret. Like the night we went to the Gatsby Ball. I spent hours the evening before working to get my eye makeup just right for him. The next evening provided an existential meltdown at the hand of fake eyelashes. Then came the party. I felt like a princess the way he adoringly stared, and we trembled as we held hands to dance. I taught him how to swing dance that night, and he taught me to stop overthinking for a few minutes.

Another Polaroid is of us on a beach for three hours knee deep in thought and neck deep in quicksand. Yet another is of the Christmas gift he gave me, and the moment where I knew I cared for him as more than just a friend. It was a few days before Christmas and we were in the middle of a McDonald's. He nervously placed his hand on the back of his neck rubbing it like he would with a slight blush on his cheeks. He handed me a small book of poems by Robert Frost, mentioning that he remembered me saying in passing how Frost was my favorite author. Additionally, there was a mixed CD of songs for me to listen to on my Christmas travels up north with a track-by-track explanation of each song and the emotions he hoped I would feel for each one. Thoughtfulness is my love language, and he knocked it out of the park on this gift. Looking in his eyes that night I knew I was falling for him. Oddly, that snapshot memory is like a snowglobe, something I'd place on a shelf and enjoy looking at every once in a while, but at peace knowing that it is not my current reality. All relationships are marked by snapshot memories, both good and bad. Some snapshots are of stains that we'd like to erase but that are needed to develop character and clarity.

There was always the pressure for "more," to move more deeply into the relationship. I recall the day I met the family and faced rounds of twenty questions from his parents as well as the curiosity of his sisters. Another time a dinner invitation from his aunt included an inquisitive request to know what kind of engagement ring I would desire. There is a line between pursuing and pressure, and Fitz had passed that line miles before. Yet I was young and naive...and he was persistent...and I liked the attention.

God did try to separate us—whether it was our constant spats or the fact that he finished school and could not find even an entry-level job, causing him to move over two hours away. It was on our last day together when things broke down.

He was to move the next day, so we planned a day doing everything we loved to do. We went to Lamplighter Coffee in

Carytown, made a photography stop in local abandoned mines, had his first experience with sushi, and topped it off watching *Frozen*, where even in the movie God was trying to tell me not to fall for the wrong guy. Then came time to say goodbye. He held me in his arms for half an hour. Tears cascaded down his face as he expressed his true feelings. I had known for some time that he loved me, and I knew the night he gave me that book of poems that I cared for him beyond friendship, but it was the first time in which we didn't walk around what we had been holding back for nearly a year. The silence said far more than words in the chill of that January evening. Then I left.

I knew the relationship was wrong, that God didn't want me with him. I knew everything I had fallen into was worldly and not pursuing God. Just because we were both Christians didn't mean we were truly pursing Him together. I tried to put a stop to it after that night, using the excuse of the distance, but we both knew we were not *just* friends any longer. I remember sobbing and fighting on the phone with him that next morning. Yet he continued to persist in pursuing me, and I let him.

We mailed each other handwritten letters multiple times a week. His letters contained pleadings to become more serious and reminders of the closeness we shared. I kept them in a box for years. There must have been over thirty letters from him all saturated with reminders of our relationship, of inside jokes, of the life we shared. As much as I loved being pursued, there was an inner gut feeling that this was not what God intended for me.

Things became even more serious after that, mainly because I ignored that gut feeling. I visited him two hours away where he lived, and he visited me in Richmond. Each time was marked with a more serious move—deeper talks, more inner heart revelations, more emotional intimacy, and so many near misses of a physical relationship beyond holding hands. After seeing *Captain America* where the storyline of Steve and Peggy had me crying, Fitz gave me an ultimatum: we would date with the goal of marriage or would stop all contact.

I planned to say yes. In fact, I wrote him a letter sharing that I had not gotten a clear no (well, it wasn't written in the sky), and so why not? But the morning came for me to tell him, and God hit me over the head so hard I had never had such a headache. It was clearly spoken to my heart that I would not receive the man God had for me if I said yes to Fitz. With that, I said no.

I suddenly saw things in full clarity, learning the complete truth of who I was to him. I felt alone and so cruel for breaking his heart. I told him the truth—that God had given me a dream many years prior of the man I was to marry, and it wasn't Fitz. Sadly, he did not believe me, though it was completely true. That conversation still to this day echoes like ghosts in the catacombs of my memory. He implied that I shouldn't contact him unless I was dying (which at that time was an actual possibility due to my health issues) and we said goodbye.

Fitz had every right in the world to be angry with me and to cut me off. It took me years to understand how we had found ourselves in such a conundrum, but what is astounding is that, when I was at the bottom of the hole I had dug myself into, God threw down a rope so I could climb out. Two years after our breakup, I contacted Fitz to apologize. Guilt over hurting him was something I could not seem to shake, and we had a kind conversation expressing forgiveness for all the wrongs we collectively brought to the table. Several years later a prayerful hope I had for him came to pass—he found the woman who was meant for him, and they soon had their first-born son. It was a hope I had years ago as my heart was shattered at ending us.

I will admit I was angry with God for months after the split. Dating Fitz served as something important in my life, and now it was gone without anything to take his place. I spent a mission trip trying to find out the truth about that dream God had given me about my future husband. I went off the deep end and began hanging out with less than noble people and making poor decisions. I learned that the sole message in an alcohol bottle is emptiness. I truly became Jonah after completing his mission—angry and bitter at God. But it was there that He came to reach me.

It was December 22 and I woke up in tears. I wanted to kill myself. I didn't want to be on this earth anymore, but it was in that bottom pit that I saw the Light when I looked up. In tearful surrender, I fell to my knees asking God to come save me. I told Him that every single time I tried to figure it out myself or do it my way, I ended up alone and in regret, so I asked Him to take back the pilot's seat, and He did. Instantly the Holy Spirit overcame me like the gentle fall of rain. I was blanketed in peace and love, and I felt no shame anymore, no regret. I was on the right path.

The weeks that followed were full of revelations and pure grace. It took my surrendering Fitz to gain the truth. It took me handing God a stone to receive a pearl of hope. The months and years that passed that fateful day have been quite an adventure. He pruned me and sanctified me as Jesus said He would.

> "I am the true vine, and my Father is the gardener. He cuts off every branch in me that bears no fruit, while every branch that does bear fruit he prunes so that it will be even more fruitful. You are already clean because of the word I have spoken to you. Remain in me, and I will remain in you. No branch can bear fruit by itself; it must remain in the vine. Neither can you bear fruit unless you remain in me." (John 15:1–4)

He pruned even the seemingly good aspects of me so I would become more fruitful later on. At the time, though, I yelled and screamed and protested for it hurts when you are torn apart.

He tore me down in order to restore me to greater glory for His purpose, and for that I am truly and eternally grateful.

That is the Romans 8:28 of this story. I deserved to be shamed by God for my direct disobedience. I deserved to be cast out and not receive the promise, but He remained faithful. The time that followed was no easy journey, but it produced the primary character of the woman I have become. Romans 5:2–5 shares, "And we rejoice in the hope of the glory of God. Not only so, but we also rejoice in our sufferings, because we know that suffering produces perseverance; perseverance, character; and character, hope. And hope does not disappoint us, because God has poured out his love into our hearts by the Holy Spirit, whom he has given us."

My point is this: the journey is worth it, because of Him. Not because of the promise of a husband, or even the person you will become, but it is worth it because of Jesus Christ Himself. For He is far greater than anything that we use to try to heal the holes in our hearts. We use a temporary Band-Aid, but find that unseen bacteria makes the infection far worse. It is through His healing blood that we are truly made whole and clean again. I cannot promise it will be easy, but it will be worth it. Romans 8:28 makes that clear: "And we know that in all things God works for the good of those who love him, who have been called according to his purpose."

A FEW MORE FROGS

It is a huge rarity to find someone who does not have a few funny or major fail dating stories in their past, but they are always hilarious nevertheless. Perhaps something here will serve as a reminder that if you have gone on a bad date, you are not alone.

My personal "frog story" is a date with a guy named Blake. I met Blake at my good friend's wedding a few years back. At the rehearsal dinner, I was attempting to stay awake after a long day of wedding venue setup when in walks in Captain America's double. He was tall, handsome, and had a smile that could melt a popsicle in a blizzard. He wasn't in the wedding so he didn't sit with the wedding party, and directly after dinner we were rushed over to the hotel. I got my chance to talk with him, though, just after the wedding.

The wedding was in the beautiful Virginia countryside and, being an amateur photographer, I took the opportunity to snatch some pictures after the official photos were finished. As I was walking back, I saw him playing cornhole with his friend. For those of you unfamiliar with cornhole, it's a game where you toss bean bags into a wooden pallet to score points. I stink at it usually. He smiled back at me and invited me to play, as I blushingly admitted to my poor coordination with such sports. In the most suave moment of my entire life, I threw the bag and it hit the target the first time, catching Blake's interest. Being coy, I shrugged it off as beginner's luck. We were interrupted by the cutting of the cake when he began inquiring about me, how I knew the bride and groom, among other things. It was soon time to leave, and he asked how to contact me. Now I never give my number out to guys—just a solid rule I have. So, I told him to find me on Facebook, quite a challenge for someone with a name like Cally.

Sure enough, within two hours a friend request sat in my inbox and we were set to go out on our first date the next week. I drove back up from college (it was my senior year) and we met at the movies. This is where his first foul ball came into play: he made me pay my own way, and he wouldn't let me choose the movie. Regardless, it was a decent time. I honestly do not even recall the movie, that's how unremarkable it was. Afterward we walked to TGI Friday's where he insisted that we sit indoors, at the bar, and I froze. At least he bought my iced tea. It was a date with good enough conversation and all, so I agreed to a second date and gave a good old-fashioned side-hug goodbye.

He would text me constantly and was very forward, but I brushed it off thinking that I was too apprehensive because I had been alone so much, and figured it was sweet. He promised to take me to one of the nicest French restaurants in town, something I certainly did not expect (I love Applebee's, honestly), but of course I said that would be lovely. I wore the cutest little sundress I had and spruced up my long brown hair and met him downtown. He proceeded to share that he wasn't that hungry after all and, after walking around aimlessly for half an hour, suggested just ice cream. I said that was fine, though I hadn't eaten since lunch and was pretty hungry. The conversation on that date was a lot less pleasurable. He dropped how he had his grandmother's jewelry and if I "was good" maybe I would get some of that. The conversation was pretty one-sided, and to top it off when I asked what his plans later were he proceeded to tell me he was going to Hooters, "Because I like their wings, wink." I asked if he was serious, and he was! I left. I got home and saw he had some bogus Facebook post about what a great date he had been on and now he was enjoying wings, and I resolved to stop dating body builders. The moral of my story is, don't settle for shallow jerks, no matter how nice they look.

ONE MORE FROG...

The last frog story I will share is a little comical, and perhaps it will make you laugh or relate.

The first date I ever went on was with one of the kindest guys I've ever known. He had an odd approach of asking me out, though; he told me he was getting a group together to go to a nearby state park, but when he came to pick me up it was just us two. I counted it as nervousness on his end for not clearly saying it was a date. Although we had a good time, it was clear to us both that we were more like brother and sister than compatible for pursuing something romantic, and to this day a decade later he remains one of my best friends.

About five years later his brother, Tim, was in town, but this story was not as sweet. Tim told me that he was planning on gathering some friends to see fireworks down by the river and asked if I could join them as well. Loving fireworks as I do, I gleefully agreed. I will admit I was not sad to spend time with Tim either, as he was kind on the eyes. When he picked me up in his 1990s pickup truck it was just him. He told me that others could not join us, and for about thirty seconds I believed him. I actually went to the restroom to text my friend asking if she had been invited, and she had no idea what I was talking about, so it was clear Tim had borrowed from his older brother's playbook of getting girls to go out with them without being honest. Nonetheless, it was one of the best dates I had ever been on. We laughed, shared so many stories, and enjoyed fireworks that were romantic in a Disney kind of way. A husband and wife wanted us to take their photo and asked if we were engaged. It was a strange question, but I suppose we looked very comfortable. In a rare occurrence, I went home that night with a broad grin on my face.

About an hour after arriving home a text came in from a friend explaining that she had found out that Tim had a girlfriend. A serious one. Yet he had taken me out on a date that very night. I felt so offended. So exploited. So insulted.

I can look at it now and shrug that I dodged a bullet, but it was still unkind of him. Yet it also helped me realize that I am worth so much more than how he treated me, and the same can be said for the girlfriend he cheated on.

In the dating pond, frogs are easily found and princes are a rarity. Yet it is worth waiting and trusting and remaining steadfast that indeed your prince is out there somewhere. Don't believe for one moment that you are worthy of a wart-encrusted amphibian when you are a daughter of the King of the universe. We deserve far more than we readily recognize.

DON'T SETTLE FOR THE BOWL OF SOUP

We live in an age of instant gratification. I too am guilty of wanting what I want when I want it, which is why I settled for the iPhone 8 Plus over the X, so I could get it a month early, and then ended up trying to sell it because it wasn't worth it. I settled for what I could grab easily, rather than the prize. But life isn't about phones.

This desire for instant gratification is nothing new. In fact, there is someone in the Bible who gave up his happiness in life for what was easily attainable.

In Genesis 25 we read the story of Jacob and Esau:

Once when Jacob was cooking some stew, Esau came in from the open country, famished. He said to Jacob, "Quick, let me have some of that red stew! I'm famished!"…

Jacob replied, "First sell me your birthright."

"Look, I am about to die," Esau said. "What good is the birthright to me?"

But Jacob said, "Swear to me first." So he swore an oath to him, selling his birthright to Jacob.

Then Jacob gave Esau some bread and some lentil stew. He ate and drank, and then got up and left. So Esau despised his birthright. (Genesis 25:29–34)

Esau saw what was quick and easily satisfying, and foolishly gave up his birthright. In their society, birthrights were a big deal, and he didn't value it at all. In the same way, don't we squander important aspects of our own lives, by going for what is easily attainable and will satisfy for a time, only to find down the road that it was all in vain?

That applies with relationships as well. When everyone seems to be pairing up and you can't go on Facebook without seeing another engagement or baby announcement, it can be so tempting to grab at what is easily attained. It can be so easy to sell our birthrights and lose out on future joy.

Think about it this way: does soup taste better when cooked in a microwave or simmered in a slow cooker? Be honest.

Relationships are like slow cookers; the longer you wait for the ultimate, the better it will be—and so worth the wait. Don't sell out for the microwave marriage that is built from sloppy leftovers and leaves you with an aftertaste of "good enough."

God has different paths and stories for us all. He has seasons for doors to open, and if your season is early on, there is nothing wrong with that whatsoever. What I am getting at here is do not settle. It's never worth it. Esau settled for a bowl of stew over an honored life.

More than likely you know if you are settling, even if you won't admit it out loud. There's that gut feeling deep down that you're selling out for that stew, when holding out a little longer would be so much more worth it. So why do we settle for less than God's best? Is it the fear of being alone? Is it the lack of faith that God actually does have someone for us? Is it that we don't trust God deep down?

What if it's all of the above?

A good friend of mine once said that when God plants these seeds of desires within our hearts, it is good, for He is good. But in our human nature, we grow impatient that it's not in our timing but in His. So, we get frustrated and angry at Him. We are disappointed and feel that He has let us down. It is natural in our humanness to resist God's ways and wrestle with Him, but it's as we listen to Him and let Him work that the real growth comes. See, it's a process, and if we just surrender and allow Him to work in us, we realize He is not cruel for making us wait. He is not slow to fulfill as we humans would count slowness; rather He is working by transforming us in our inner being for our highest good and His greatest glory. Don't resist the transformation. Don't settle for the stew.

Personally, I too was on the path to settling. It's easy to look around and see all your friends getting married and in this sort of dreamland, and then you start to doubt that you're worthy of that happiness. So, you settle. You begin in your heart to settle for what you know is not God's best, or your best. You convince yourself that you are actually too picky and that your aspirations are far too high, and you convince yourself that you're worth so little. Don't do this. Don't settle for good enough. Consider what could be if you were bold enough to trust in God's answer for what He says is His best for you.

Dear Lord,

Please work in us. Please help us to be patient and never settle for a bowl of soup, but instead wait for what You have for us. Help us to surrender to Your timing and Your call. We know You always reward obedience, in Your time, not ours.

In Jesus' name,

Amen.

CHAPTER 6

In the Waiting

ACTIVE WAITING

Active waiting sounds like an oxymoron. The act of patiently waiting, yet being active, may sound foreign to some. In cycling classes (think SoulCycle) there is a term "active recovery," which is where one recovers from a massive climb without stopping. In the same way, it is possible to actively be patient. It is possible to intentionally, actively wait.

Being intentional is a way of life. It puts the One you serve first, and it makes an effort to in every way mold your life to focus on Christ, with every action. James 5:12 calls to "let your 'Yes' be yes, and your 'No,' no." This means intentionally living in such a way that you make the choice to let the major and minor decisions of your life reflect and honor God in every way. Living with intention will always yield abundant fruit, for even if we make mistakes God is working with that spirit, that heart, and those intentions to bless the Kingdom, and in turn He will bless you. James 5:16 shares, "The prayer of a righteous man is powerful and effective." God is able to look past our masks, past the walls we put up, and look into the deep intentions of our spirits. When we live in such an intentional way as to bless Him, He supplies where we lack, He guides, He blesses. Even in the waiting periods of life.

If God has called you into a season of waiting, it is never for you to just sit like Rapunzel in a tower waiting for a prince. In fact, it is in those waiting seasons that the most work can take place. The greatest activity can occur. The root-defining growth can happen.

Keep in mind that the root determines the fruit. The deeper the root, the more abundant the fruit will be. Jesus speaks of it in the parable of the sower:

> "Listen! A farmer went out to plant some seeds. As he scattered them across his field, some seeds fell on a footpath, and the birds came and ate them. Other seeds fell on shallow soil with underlying rock. The seeds sprouted quickly because the soil was shallow. But the plants soon wilted under the hot sun, and since they didn't have deep roots, they died. Other seeds fell among thorns that grew up and choked out the tender plants. Still other seeds fell on fertile soil, and they produced a crop that was thirty, sixty, and even a hundred times as much as had been planted! Anyone with ears to hear should listen and understand." (Matthew 13:3–9, NLT)

The seeds with the deep roots produced an exponential crop. This is what waiting and enduring will accomplish when done right. When you intentionally seek to wait actively, your roots will deepen and the fruit will be far more abundant. It is surprising how gardening will indeed prove these verses true. I am reminded of a story a dear friend shared with me recently. She explained how last year she planted some seeds, making sure they weren't too close to the surface and had plenty of opportunity for sun and water. Week after week, nothing sprouted up. She kept tending to it daily but it seemed to no avail. One day she had the thought to brush away the dirt, and she discovered that the plant had actually been growing the entire time. Not only had it been growing, but its roots went very, very deep. The plant didn't show on the surface, but the roots were ensuring that it would last for years to come. It had such deep roots that even the strongest of storms would not harm the plant.

It's the same way with our lives. We may pray about something for even years on end and feel we have nothing on the outside to show for it, but take into consideration that God has planted some seed. He is growing the roots in the situation, and He is growing your roots in Him. Don't give up just because you can't see it—remember, the deeper the root, the stronger the tree. This is active waiting.

Think of it like a hallway. If you are in that hallway between seasons, you can actively wait and create something beautiful. Paint the hallways, use the time to express yourself as creatively as possible. Take hold of the blank canvas of time and create something unique in every way. That is how this book was made. I've been in an active waiting season for some time now, but what is humbling is that God has taken this time to not only grow my roots richly in Him, but to create. Time to create meaningful and intentional relationships with other women (my little "flock of birds" I mentor) and time to richly enjoy the golden days of doing life with my friends. This book was inspired by their challenges and questions, as well as a few of my own. If it were not for this waiting period God has given me, this would never have been written.

Active waiting is a time in which the work behind the scenes, the work deep within can flourish. Don't just endure such a season, richly bloom within its borders.

Prayer

Dear Lord,
Thank You for knowing better than us. Thank You that even
in those seasons where we resist with all of our flesh, You know
better. You know that such seasons can be used to actively grow,
actively learn, and actively flourish within You. Help us to live
with intention, help us when we lack, and let each and every
season in our lives be used for Your glory and our benefit—to
know You all the more.
In Christ's name,
Amen.

DEAR FUTURE HUSBAND

Perhaps what you are specifically waiting for is more of a *who* than a *what*: a future husband. The blessing is that you can actively wait for your husband as well. This doesn't merely mean avoiding dating those fleshly relationships that you know for certain are not of God, but also communicating your heart to your husband before you even meet him.

For a decade, I've been writing letters to my future husband. They began in a journal, then two journals, then slews of letters. The running total right now is around two hundred and fifty... I've been actively waiting for a while. What is beautiful is what those letters hold. They have the ability to convey my heart, intent, and growth throughout the years. From milestones he wasn't there for to ideas for apple trees at our home to sincere written prayers for him—they're all there. I like to imagine how beautiful it will be the day he reads them. The day he sees how intentionally God led me to pray for him, to think of him, to love him before we even met. It is like a time capsule I can hand him one day.

These letters can be a style that is all your own too. They can be in prayer form, diary form, or anything you want. You can wait to fill his name in later for the "Dear _____" part, or simply put, "Dear Future Husband." Make the letters your own. They are a lovely representation of conveying your heart to his heart, one letter at a time.

Often we experience memories, milestones, or events that we really wish we could share with a significant other, but that person is not in your life yet. So I have written him letters with such detail that he feels as if he were there as it happened. I want him to know even before he was part of my life that he held a seat at the table, and that all the thousands of little details I would forget were not carried away in the winds of time. They abide right there in chicken-scratch handwriting just for him.

Another topic I think is good to share in these messages is how you are really feeling. Vulnerability opens the door to intimacy and by the time he reads these tender-hearted musings you will be bound by God, where intimacy is safe to flourish and abide. Perhaps recording for your future husband a moment of loneliness, a behind-the-scenes look at your life, or an aching heart can be a soft landing place for your weary heart.

Especially do not forget to write such letters leading up to your wedding as well. Save these letters forever, and one day when you are both graying and life is hard, you can recall that fresh, bright-eyed love that was bottled up for a time, like a fine wine. Savored, saved, and significant solely for him.

Dear Lord,

Thank You for the future spouse of each young woman reading this book. We pray for him even now. We pray that the heart of the woman reading this will patiently wait for him, pray for him,

and truly know that he is worth waiting for. We pray for his heart for You; we pray that daily he picks up his cross and follows You. We pray that he is growing and becoming the mighty man of Christ You intended him to be. We pray for the letters that will be written for his heart from his loving wife.
In Jesus' name,
Amen.

RUTH BEFORE BOAZ

This section is for the girls with a heart like Ruth.

Ruth wasn't just a typical woman. She faced adversity, loss, grief, and heartache but remained steadfast and faithful through it all. She knew that her God would be faithful to her...and He was.

Ruth's story begins with a life-chapter ending. Her husband of ten years suddenly dies along with her brother-in-law and father-in-law. Ruth, Naomi (her mother-in-law), and Orpah (her sister-in-law, who I picture in my head as Oprah) are all left widows. The secure and safe life they had come to know was shattered. They must have felt so lonely, forgotten, and unsure of where to go next. Naomi even said her new nickname should be "Mara," which means "bitter." Orpah decides to go back to her father's family for refuge, and Naomi suggests Ruth do the same. This time of decision is the defining moment that will create a domino effect for the rest of Ruth's life. You see, she did not see her role in Naomi's family to be temporary. It was not some entry-level job she was using as a stepping stone. It was not just a chapter or season in her life. Naomi was *family*. Ruth was committed to God to serve in that family until death. Let's look to the text:

"Look," said Naomi, "your sister-in-law is going back to her people and her gods. Go back with her.

But Ruth replied, "Don't urge me to leave you or to turn back from you. Where you go I will go, and where you stay I will stay. Your people will be my people and your God my God. Where you die I will die, and there I will be buried. May the LORD deal with me, be it ever so severely, if anything but death separates you and me." When Naomi realized that Ruth was determined to go with her, she stopped urging her. (Ruth 1:15–18)

This is the first lesson we can take note of from Ruth. She was loyal to where God had called her. God had chosen her to marry into Naomi's family, and Ruth saw that as a commitment until her death. She chose to faithfully live out the position God had called her to—even if it was not what others preferred or encouraged. Let's make this personal. Has there ever been a time in your own life when you knew without a doubt that God was calling you to stay or go, and you received little to no support for your decision? Perhaps everyone called you crazy for staying or going and looked down on you for that. It could mean a less comfortable life, or that hardships and storms might ensue. Perhaps it seemed the more radical choice—but it was the God-given obedience choice.

This is where Ruth was. Sure, Ruth could have gone home like Orpah did and lived a safe, quiet life back home with her parents. She would have received little to no harassment from her family or peers. It would have been a safe choice—but because Ruth was obedient to God's call even when it made no sense to those around her, she was blessed. You see, though Ruth was an ordinary woman, she served an extraordinary God who had a very important destiny for her that hinged completely on her obedience in season. Let's keep going.

She continued to live with Naomi, working hard for the necessities of life where she could. In that society, land owners would allow for those less fortunate to eat off the corners of their land. Now "it just so happened" that Ruth found herself gathering food from the property of a man named Boaz. For cinematic quality, we can imagine Boaz as a silver fox. Not the youngest man, but certainly still a man who could make your heart flutter when he beams a million-dollar smile. In my head, he has the enduring good looks of Eric Metaxas...but I digress.

As Ruth is engaged in her daily duties of collecting food, I imagine that when she first sees Boaz all of time stops for a moment in those eyes. Boaz takes notice of her as well and inquires of her story. This is where we see their first interaction take place:

> So, Boaz said to Ruth, "My daughter, listen to me. Don't go and glean in another field and don't go away from here. Stay here with my servant girls. Watch the field where the men are harvesting, and follow along after the girls. I have told the men not to touch you. And whenever you are thirsty, go and get a drink from the water jars the men have filled."
>
> At this, she bowed down with her face to the ground. She exclaimed, "Why have I found such favor in your eyes that you notice me—a foreigner?"
>
> Boaz replied, "I've been told all about what you have done for your mother-in-law since the death of your husband—how you left your father and mother and your homeland and came to live with a people you did not know before. May the LORD repay you for what you have done. May you be richly rewarded by the LORD, the God of Israel, under whose wings you have come to take refuge."
> (Ruth 2:8–12)

At first glance this seems an odd first conversation, but when we really dig into it we see the respect Boaz gave her at first sight.

He was moved by her integrity to fulfill her commitment to Naomi's family until *her* death, not only the death of her husband. Boaz also saw the light of the Lord shining from her. By far my favorite line of Boaz is when he speaks of God "under whose wings you have come to take refuge." Gah! This is stunning. Boaz was impressed with Ruth not for her looks, but because she made the *choice* to take refuge in God. She chose to live her life in such an intentional way that she was committed to God—not the consensus of her peers—for refuge, strength, and direction. In the most respectful way Boaz can convey this, he allows Ruth to gather regularly from his fields and gives her permission to drink from his water supply. Boaz even then wanted to take care of her, not to dictate what she would do, but to offer everything he could in the most respectful way.

Ruth then goes home to Naomi to tell of her day, and Naomi is all too ready to be a good Mama and help make things happen. This next part is going to sound a little strange, but just keep with the story. It will all make sense once we flesh it out.

> One day Naomi her mother-in-law said to her, "My daughter, should I not try to find a home for you, where you will be well provided for? Is not Boaz, with whose servant girls you have been, a kinsman of ours? Tonight he will be winnowing barley on the threshing floor. Wash and perfume yourself, and put on your best clothes. Then go down to the threshing floor, but don't let him know you are there until he has finished eating and drinking. When he lies down, note the place where he is lying. Then go and uncover his feet and lie down. He will tell you what to do." (Ruth 3:1–4)

Naomi told Ruth to pursue Boaz. She noted to dress in her very best, and to sincerely and honestly go to him with her intentions.

Though it is not explicitly said, I think it is safe to assume Ruth was quite taken with Boaz, and it was Naomi's hope to encourage this relationship to happen. Now at first glance when we read verse 4, we cannot help but think it sounds a little strange. Kind of a, "Hey, I just met you, and this is crazy…but I'll lie in your bed. Marry me, maybe?" It's not as promiscuous as it sounds. Ruth was actually humbling herself by lying at Boaz's feet to show him reverence and respect. This was a risky move in itself being an unmarried woman pursuing a man of such importance, but this is evidence of God having a hand on every single detail.

God led Naomi's heart to encourage Ruth to put herself out there for Boaz, to confront him and share her own feelings, and God filled in the rest. Obedience to God may not always make sense and can often be incredibly daring and risky, but if it is from the Lord Himself it will turn out well in the end. Jesus' words ring true in this instance: "You do not realize now what I am doing, but later you will understand" (John 13:7).

Thankfully we are not left with a cliff hanger in this story. What happens next is a God-woven story of grace and blessings.

"Who are you?" he asked.

"I am your servant Ruth," she said. "Spread the corner of your garment over me, since you are a kinsman-redeemer."

"The LORD bless you, my daughter," he replied. "This kindness is greater than that which you showed earlier: You have not run after the younger men, whether rich or poor. And now, my daughter, don't be afraid. I will do for you all you ask. All my fellow townsmen know that you are a woman of noble character. Although it is true that I am near of kin, there is a kinsman-redeemer nearer than I. Stay here for the night, and in the morning if he wants to redeem, good; let him redeem. But if he is not willing, as surely as the LORD lives I will do it. Lie here until morning."

So she lay at his feet until morning, but got up before anyone could be recognized; and he said, "Don't let it be known that a woman came to the threshing floor."

He also said, "Bring me the shawl you are wearing and hold it out." When she did so, he poured into it six measures of barley and placed it on her. Then he went back to town. (Ruth 3:9–15)

There is an abundance of symbolism here. The kinsman-redeemer is a male relative who, according to various laws of the Pentateuch, had the responsibility to act on behalf of a relative who was in trouble, danger, or need. This meant acting on the behalf of the person in crisis, much like how God does for us. We are His children, and when we are in a crisis He is there to comfort and help us. Ruth had a kinsman-redeemer who was closer by law, so that is why it was even more noble of Boaz to step up and courageously ask for Ruth's hand in marriage.

Boaz again shows his upstanding morals when he had the opportunity to take advantage of Ruth by forcing himself on her, but instead he respects her. He does not defile her reputation. He shows respect by keeping her honor safe and secure. Also, note how he fed her and Naomi breakfast with all the barley he sent her off with. Bonus points.

Back at the ranch Naomi is ready to hear how things went. Ruth explains how Boaz must ask permission in order to marry her, and how he showed respect to her and her family by doing what was proper. Naomi replied, "Wait, my daughter, until you find out what happens. For the man will not rest until the matter is settled today" (Ruth 3:18). This is a reminder that at times obedience will leave us with a cliff hanger. You will have done all that you can do, but the outcome rests in the Lord's hands and He will work in the hearts of men to fulfill His purposes.

Ruth's obedience paid off. Boaz is given approval to marry her, and truly what happens next is lovelier than even the most tear-jerking Hallmark movie or greatest of fairytales.

> So Boaz took Ruth and she became his wife. Then he went to her, and the LORD enabled her to conceive, and she gave birth to a son. The women said to Naomi: "Praise be to the LORD, who this day has not left you without a kinsman-redeemer. May he become famous throughout Israel! He will renew your life and sustain you in your old age. For your daughter-in-law, who loves you and who is better to you than seven sons, has given him birth." (Ruth 4:13–15)

Boaz marries Ruth. Childless in her first marriage, God now blesses her with a beautiful son—a son who is indeed the fruit of obedience. Obedience always ushers forth a harvest, but in God's timing, not ours. We see those who witnessed this blessing humbled by the work of the Lord, even saying how this story would be made famous by the events that have taken place in Ruth and Naomi's lives.

But Ruth's story does not end here. in fact, her obedience would create a domino effect that would bless the entire universe until the end of age. You see, Ruth gave birth to a son named Obed. Obed had a son named Jesse, who had a son named David. David would be made the king over all Israel and have a heart truly after God. David would even come to see what his own great-grandfather saw in Ruth—that she had taken refuge under God's wings (Ruth 2:12)—for he later writes of God, "He will cover you with his feathers, and under his wings you will find refuge; his faithfulness will be your shield and rampart" (Psalm 91:4). The actions and heart of his ancestors had a domino effect on his own understanding and worldview. This goes to show that the obedience of one person—even one woman—can affect the course of history for the Kingdom for all time. You see, David would be in the lineage of Jesus. God knew Ruth would be obedient to the call upon her life, and He chose her for such a mission, such a life.

Do not regard your beginnings as your ending. Your story is not even finished when you leave this earth, for the impact you have on others can continue forever, just like love. A quote I came across years ago has always stuck with me: "In life be a snowflake—leave a mark, but no stain." The way you live your life and your obedience even in small things leaves marks. These marks effect those in your surroundings, and that legacy goes on and on. Do not believe your beginnings are in vain. Do not believe your obedience is in vain. God always blesses obedience, always blesses good intentions, always fulfills His purpose. It is up to us to be obedient like Ruth and trust even when the entire world seems against us.

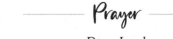

Prayer

Dear Lord,
Thank You for noble women like Ruth. Thank You that we can truly look to them as role models in pursuit of Your calling. We pray that we will have the courage and boldness to live fearlessly in service of Your call, like Ruth did. We pray for men after Your own heart like Boaz. We pray for Your glory to be shown throughout our lives.
In Jesus' name,
Amen.

CHAPTER 7

Learned Wisdom

THE HONOR OF INTERCESSION

As I mentioned in chapter 6, praying for my future spouse has indeed become a constant. I pray for him not just daily but throughout the day. After many years of this habit there have been times when my resolve grew weak and I became exhausted, quite honestly. One day I was prayer journaling and felt a very heavy and overwhelming weight upon my shoulders concerning my future husband. It drenched my mood like a wet coat, so heavy I could barely articulate words to say, let alone pray. Beset with this overcoming emotion, I was unable to shake it off as nothing. I began to pray for him, unsure what to pray. Thankfully we have the Holy Spirit as our powerful intercessor who is able to translate even moans into prayers to our heavenly Father. I was given affirmation that my prayers were not in vain.

The following day, I came to the realization that it was not a burden but a blessing for me to pray for this man. I was gifted a spiritual connection with this man to pray for him without any sign that he needed intercession. This is the vital piece to remember when you are feeling depleted and exhausted in praying for someone: it is truly an honor.

There are almost eight billion people on this planet, half of whom are women, and out of all those women, God chose me to pray for this man. Moreover, I was created for this. See, when God made the first woman, Eve, He had the first man, Adam, in mind. The Bible says, "But for Adam no suitable helper was found. So the LORD God caused the man to fall into a deep sleep; and while he was sleeping, he took one of the man's ribs and closed up the place with flesh. Then the LORD God made a woman from the rib he had taken out of the man, and he brought her to the man" (Genesis 2:20–22). God knew Adam's heart, for He was the one who made it, and He made Eve perfectly suited for Adam. The same is true of your heart, dear reader. He had a specific man in mind when He made you, and likewise you were on His mind when creating this man. What a sincere honor it is truly to pray for this man meant for you. For God had you in mind in the creation of this man, and it is your honor and duty to pray for this man in your life.

Paul writes in 1 Corinthians 7:34–35, "But a married woman is concerned about the affairs of this world—how she can please her husband. I am saying this for your own good, not to restrict you, but that you may live in a right way in undivided devotion to the Lord." A woman who has a husband (or is praying for her future husband) is naturally concerned with her man, but that doesn't mean she can't be devoted to the Lord as well. In fact, the object of a godly marriage is that, by loving your spouse, you in turn fall more deeply in love with God. So, praying for your spouse in turn blesses God. It's honestly an honor if God gives you someone to pray for.

For me, prayer is a constant, but this was not always the case. After God rejuvenated my relationship with Him, I took captive the wanderings of my mind and began to navigate such thoughts in prayer to God. I also had very intentional intercession time for my future husband. I had read many times that forty seemed to be a very holy number, such as the forty days of Noah's flood or Jesus' temptation in the desert. In praying about how to conduct my prayer time, I learned through a sermon and Scripture (Mark 6:48) that after Jesus fed the five thousand He went off to pray in the hills. He instructed the disciples to go on ahead of Him, and around 3 a.m. He came to them in the middle of the lake. It was here that the miracle of Jesus walking on water, and calling Peter out to walk on the water as well, occurred. The story of Jesus calling Peter out of the boat has always been near and dear to my heart, so I felt Jesus was calling me to come to Him at the same time. So, I set my alarm for 3 a.m. every morning and prayed for forty days. I prayed however the Spirit would lead me that day. At times, it was for my future husband's days, sometimes for his purity, other times for his parents (often his mom specifically), or perhaps that he too would be awakened at 3 a.m. with the call to just be near God. I wrote down every night what I interceded for Him, along with the verses God provided in the wee hours of the morning. The last day was actually the day of a solar eclipse, a day in which the entire world stopped for a few brief moments to see the skies proclaim God's glory, and I do not think that was a coincidence.

When I finished the forty days, I did not stop praying. In fact, I've been praying for him with many a free thought for the past few years now. I am not saying that to sound righteous, or by any means like I am perfect, but in honesty it's more for God than it is for my future husband. You see, we have the beautiful opportunity to pray for others so that they bless the Kingdom. Eric Metaxas once conveyed how the real work we do is on this side of the veil; once we are in heaven, it is all praising and no sadness. All joy. So, it is vital that on this side of heaven we strive to do as much as we can for the Kingdom. God blessed each of us with the incredible honor of being a voice in the world to those around us. I see that calling as a massive honor, but with a great weight along with it. I know my future spouse needs someone praying for him and supporting him, even from the sidelines. I cannot even imagine what all he will do in his life, but I pray over it. Your spouse is the exact same; he has a call and a place in ministry in his life. Even if he is working for a gas station, he has the beautiful call to scatter seeds for Christ. He needs prayer, and if you are his future wife, he needs you. This is the job of a rib: to support the man to be upright toward God. So, with that, let us pray.

Dear Lord,
We praise Your holy name. We know that You and You alone
can guide and instruct hearts. We pray for our future spouses that
You would guide them and work within them. We pray that in
the same way, through the intercession of others, You would work
within us as well. We give our hearts to You for changing and
molding. We give to You the hearts of our spouses for changing
and molding. We give our breath, our day, and our role on this
side of the veil for Your glory.
In Jesus' name,
Amen.

BANKS OF THE RED SEA

Where are you today? Are you holding up during one of the worst seasons of your life? Are your hopes and dreams and desires starting to seem impossible? Is everything you thought God had promised or would give you by now looking like the last thing that could happen right now? If so, you are at the banks of the Red Sea.

Nearly everyone knows the story of how God parted the Red Sea for the Israelites, but some perhaps don't know all the massive details that went into this miracle. See, after a long season of negotiations—specifically through ten plagues—the Pharaoh of Egypt finally allowed the Israelites to go free. Approximately two million of them headed out for the Promised Land of Canaan, but after such a victory there was another issue up around the river bend (Pocahontas reference).

Exodus 14:1–4 tells us,

> Then the LORD said to Moses, "Tell the Israelites to turn back and encamp near Pi Hahiroth, between Migdol and the sea. They are to encamp by the sea, directly opposite Baal Zephon. Pharaoh will think, 'The Israelites are wandering around the land in confusion, hemmed in by the desert.' And I will harden Pharaoh's heart, and he will pursue them. But I will gain glory for myself through Pharaoh and all his army, and the Egyptians will know that I am the LORD." So, the Israelites did this.

This means that the original planned route was altered so that it would become more difficult, but God was setting them up for a miracle. Pharaoh's heart was hardened, and he decided not to just let all his slaves leave, not after all the plagues Egypt had seen trying to hold on to them so firmly. Moses led the caravan of these two million people and they found themselves at the banks of the Red Sea. Now, the Red Sea is no tiny pond one can wade through or hop over; it is a massive body of water. To make matters more difficult, an entire army of hot-headed Egyptians were on their tails. These Israelites had all grown up as slaves, not trained warriors, so they had no idea how to fight an army. With no weapons, they saw the choices before them as either drown or die by the sword. They felt abandoned.

How often are we metaphorically in this spot? Where it seems there is no way out, no option in which we come out the other side? At times, we may even find ourselves screaming at God for leading us down this path where everything is in disarray. Perhaps we saw the first leg of success and rejoiced in His faithfulness only to turn around and find everything looks ten times worse than before. You are not the first to have such thoughts. The Israelites even asked if the sole reason God brought them out to the desert was that there was more room for graves out there (see Exodus 14:11). But God wasn't finished yet.

Moses, the leader of this group at the time, received his orders from God. Moses knew God and had seen His power and sovereignty in his life, so he knew there would be a way out. He assured the Israelites, "Do not be afraid. Stand firm and you will see the deliverance the LORD will bring you today. The Egyptians you see today you will never see again. The LORD will fight for you; you need only to be still" (Exodus 14:13–14). Then just as everything looked as hopeless as ever, God came through. He told Moses to merely stretch out his hand over the sea (which I'm sure Moses was very confused with), and then before their eyes the Red Sea parted.

The entire group of about two million men, women, and children walked across not in mud but on dry land. On each side was a skyscraper of water as they passed through the sea. Then as the Egyptians behind them attempted to cross, the waters fell upon them and they were wiped out. God took care of each and every single one. He kept true to His word that not only would the Israelites see who God was but so would the Egyptians. God protects His own.

God is never changing; His character remains steadfast forever. This was as true in the New Testament times as it is today. Jesus says in John 13:7, "You do not realize now what I am doing, but later you will understand." We can also see in Romans 8:28, "And we know that in all things God works for the good of those who love him, who have been called according to his purpose."

We may not get the Red Sea parting every single time, but we can know that God will indeed work all things together for our good and His purpose and glory. How beautiful is that?

I write this as a reminder to myself. Last week I found myself weeping at the banks of the Red Sea. Feeling confused and lost on this journey on which God has asked me to trust and follow Him, I realized that He came through for people who trusted and followed Him before, so He will do it again. 1 Samuel 15:29 says that God "is not a man, that he should change his mind," and we can hold on to that promise. He is who He says He is, and just as His eye is on a sparrow, His eye is on us too.

Prayer

Dear Lord,
We stand here today at the banks of the Red Sea. You led us here,
just as You once led the people of Israel here too. Lord, in that day
long ago You remembered Your promise, and You came through.
You saved a nation that day for Your glory, and we pray that in
this moment You would come through for us. Let us never forget
Your promises or provisions, rather let us hold firmly to the belief
that You are working all things together for Your glory and our
benefit, whether this sea parts or not.
In Jesus' name,
Amen.

OLIVE TREES

It has become such an unfortunate stereotype of so-called Christians that all Christianity is about is a bunch of angry, judgmental people with self-righteous attitudes. What they neglect to understand is that the Bible is completely full of fallen and very much human people just like you and me. I could rant for hours upon this subject, but here I'd like to dive into a certain psalm David poured out.

David was renowned for being a man after God's own heart. From a young age, he stood in faith to defeat a literal giant with a mere slingshot, and as a teen was told that he would one day be king over all Israel. His life was full of uncertainties throughout, but what is most compelling is his heart expressed throughout the psalms.

David penned half of the psalms, many of which are songs full of ever-changing emotions. I certainly doubt I am the only one who can relate. One of the most incredible is Psalm 52:

> But I am like an olive tree flourishing in the house of God; I trust in God's unfailing love for ever and ever. I will praise you forever for what you have done; in your name I will hope, for your name is good. I will praise you in the presence of your saints. (Psalm 52:8–9)

In all of creation, the olive tree is one of the longest living and enduring trees. David felt like an olive tree flourishing in the deep roots of God. Christ speaks of the meaning of roots later in Mark 4:8: "Still other seed fell on good soil. It came up, grew and produced a crop, multiplying thirty, sixty, or even a hundred times."

Jesus speaks further of what it means to produce an abundant crop in John 15:

"I am the true vine, and my Father is the gardener. He cuts off every branch in me that bears no fruit, while every branch that does bear fruit he prunes so that it will be even more fruitful ... Remain in me, and I will remain in you." (John 15:1–4)

This passage is saying that, just like David, we are branches living in Jesus, the vine. God is the Gardener and lovingly prunes and refines us. The seasons of this pruning are painful, tedious, and excruciating at times, but achieve a greater purpose. Just like an olive tree bears much fruit, when we abide in the true vine and are deeply rooted in Christ, we can know that the seasons of pruning are not in vain. Rather, these seasons ensure that in the harvest season the crop will be plentiful.

Malachi 3:10–12 says:

"Test me in this," says the LORD Almighty, "and see if I will not throw open the floodgates of heaven and pour out so much blessing that you will not have room enough for it. I will prevent pests from devouring your crops, and the vines in your fields will not cast their fruit," says the LORD Almighty. "Then all the nations will call you blessed, for yours will be a delightful land."

I am not saying that we are to walk into these pruning seasons in hopes of an abundance of tangible blessings; rather, the fruit we bear is often spiritual. I do believe we walk out of such seasons with an abundance of the Spirit within us. A closeness, an abiding, a rooting so deep within God that it is a peace unknown and unachievable by any other way.

Let us pray to be like King David, deeply rooted in Him like an olive tree. Let us pray to be a flourishing olive tree and know that the pruning seasons will bear an abundance of fruit. The fruit of peace. The fruit of love. The fruit of truth. All the fruit of the Holy Spirit, the greatest reward we receive in this life.

Prayer

Dear Lord,
Make us like an olive tree, deeply rooted in You. Grow us, prune
us, destine us to flourish for Your glory. May we stand apart from
the rest of the world, so that others may see Your glory through
our lives. Lord, make us fruitful, and guide us as we endure the
pruning to Your liking.
In Jesus' name,
Amen.

GOD'S PLAN VS. OURS

So, you have followed Psalm 37:4, delighting yourself in the LORD and fully surrendering your heart to Him. He has planted within your heart a dream, a vision, a hope for your future. You think the path to that will be smooth, easy, and quick, but all at once you find that is not the case. You begin to grow confused, doubtful, and possibly a little angry at all the struggles, but what if there is something greater in store for you than merely getting from A to B? What if climbing this mountain will prove far greater than just reaching the finish line? What if by the end of it you're a different person entirely? Stick with me now…

It may be the most common cliché to compare life's journey to climbing a mountain, but when was the last time anyone actually took a hike up a mountain? One Saturday a group of us from my church went to climb Spy Rock, a three-mile uphill hike that peaks at about a 3,800-foot elevation. I prayed before we left that God would teach me something this day, and boy, did He ever.

We started out the morning in pouring rain, unsure of the conditions that awaited us two hours away but with optimistic hearts and an idealistic hope that the day would prove sunny. It did. The hike started off as a simple nature trail, but then was met with steep hills and rocks. I'm not going to lie, I felt winded after the first quarter mile of a steep uphill climb and was severely regretting that I'd gone to the gym only three times a week this summer and not daily like I did in the spring. Nevertheless, I kept going. Soon the trail became a lot harder and steeper. The thing was, the first part of the trail had conditioned me so by the time I got to the more challenging spots, the beginning seemed like a walk in the park (literally). Then came the real challenge: scaling the rock to the top.

I have taken one rock climbing class, and halfway scaled a rock once before, so this was pretty new. Looking up at the top, part of me wanted to give up and head back to where I began without victory, a story, or success. Something in our spirits wants to give up at the eleventh hour, doesn't it? Something within us wants to walk away even though we have endured so much and worked so hard, for many reasons, but mainly because we are exhausted or fearful. Yet I endured.

I took it slow and steady, but I scaled that giant rock of a mountain. Taking risks and holding my breath, I quickly made it to the top. And was it ever worth it!

The view was incredible, to see how far I had come and to view all of God's glory in creation surrounding us. A plethora of green filled our view. Suddenly being tired didn't matter, nor did how long it had taken to get to the top. It no longer mattered that I experienced anxiety halfway up either. Then came the best part.

Of all the things I love in God's creation, a bird tops the list. Birds amaze me; their freedom, their beauty, their ability to swiftly navigate the sky. Up there on Spy Rock I felt like a bird, especially because the rock was engulfed by a cloud. We saw the cloud hover near us and suddenly embrace us within its billowy fog. The smell after rain is deemed "petrichor," and that happens to be my favorite word for it is my favorite smell. This topped even summer's most glorious after-rain smell, with a fragrance of peaceful dew and pure vapor. Our heads were literally in the clouds, and for a brief moment I was like one of the birds.

Reflecting later, I realized God brought me through today's experience to show me what He has done, what He is doing, and what He will do. It is applicable to just about any journey, but I knew the specifics He was pointing out for me here. The journey may start out rocky, but endurance produces perseverance and suddenly the beginning seems minuscule compared to what occurs when you're really going. That perseverance produces character when the eleventh-hour strikes and you want to give up and turn back. And that character produces hope, hope that once you're at the top, it will all have been worth it. Indeed it was, and indeed it will be. Worth every step, every stumble, every ounce of stamina. The greatest reward of all is that journeys create for us a chance to know Christ better. A chance to learn more about who He really is and what we are really made of. The best part is, that relationship and that understanding of Him is so glorious, the view from the top pales in comparison, but is brought even more vibrantly alive by its accompaniment. Keep climbing, friend.

Prayer

Dear Lord,
Though we make so many plans, often they are changed.
We know that You see our plans and change them to,
in actuality, be perfect—in Your perfect will for us. Lord,
we give these plans and goals and aspirations to You so that
You may have the control and say in our lives.
We praise You, oh Lord.
In Jesus' name,
Amen.

UNDER GOD'S WING

Spiritual warfare is real. It is war. It can be overwhelming. It is not hopeless. It is worth it.

In my walk as a Christian, I have met a number of Christians who have never really experienced an attack of the enemy that was not in the form of what we commonly think of as temptation. In Matthew 4 we see Jesus being tempted by the enemy, but what did this actually mean? Mainstream culture will describe temptation in layman's terms as something we ought not to do, but are lured with a compelling carrot into nearly or actually doing. This is something the enemy will quite often whip up to distract us from our God-given missions or to get us to fall yet again to our flesh. What is often overlooked, but actually very prevalent, is another form of temptation: an attack from the enemy.

These temptations were seen in Matthew 4 as well when the enemy fought against Jesus. They are seen in Daniel 10 when the angel sent to assist Daniel took twenty-one days to fight through the warfare before he could reach Daniel. These attacks are packed with anxiety, fear, paranoia, and a sense of inadequacy. They will seek to convince a person that God is a liar, just as the enemy convinced Eve that God was fooling her. These attacks will create a cyclone of confusion and doubt swirling about as we are left clinging to the wreckage all within our own heads. In these circumstances, below are verses to discern what is God and what is not, and how to fight back:

- "God is not a God of disorder but of peace" (1 Corinthians 14:33).
- "Perfect love drives out fear" (1 John 4:18).
- "Cast all your anxiety on him because he cares for you" (1 Peter 5:7).
- "In this world you will have trouble. But take heart! I have overcome the world" (John 16:33).

Consider Job. He was actually the most upright and righteous man in the world when the enemy sought to attack his life. Satan had to approach God to ask if he could attack Job, because nothing is permitted to hit us without His permission, but it leads to the question, why would a kind and loving God allow this? The answer is simply: so we will lean on Him. You see, Job was attacked on everything he had. His financial livelihood was ruined, his health deteriorated, and he even lost all of his children on the same day. I look at these and correlate them within my own life of job loss, health issues, or the loss of someone I loved more than life. Job in truth is my kindred spirit. As usual with humans, our friends always have their two cents to interject. Job's friends visited him and for a period just sat silently, unsure of what to say. Then they began to explain that Job must have sinned in some way, and that this suffering was what he deserved. One told Job to turn his back on God entirely and give up hope. Another friend had a different approach, and just stated the truth that God is a mystery, bigger than we can comprehend, so we shouldn't try to. Job felt alone, broken, confused, and like he was the last person on earth who believed God still had hope for his life. Then God showed up. The key here is that it was not anything that Job earned. Job didn't burn so many sacrifices that he earned enough brownie points to capture the attention of God, nor did he figure out his life. He simply sought God and waited.

And God did more than just show up. He showed His sovereignty and power. Think about that—Job had a personal encounter with the living God who created the entire universe. Job endured the storms, he clung to God, and none of it was in vain. Not a stitch, not a tear, not a prayer in vain. Then coming like a thunderous roar God spoke and showed that He was there the entire time. Not a second passed without God being present. The story has a happy ending in that God actually blessed Job double what he had before—He even paid him back exponentially through his life, as Job lived to be one hundred and forty. Though possessions, health, and children are blessings, Job received the greatest reward in knowing God personally.

Job isn't the only one who saw that He is our greatest reward and treasure. Hannah, the mother of Samuel, saw this firsthand as well. The Bible recalls that "in bitterness of soul Hannah wept much" at the altar as she prayed (1 Samuel 1:10). She ached for a son, and though it was not an attack of the enemy per se, she had "great anguish and grief" (v. 16). Then God blesses her, and within a short time she did indeed have her son. What is beautiful in her prayer in 1 Samuel 2 is that she praises God for who He is far more than for what He gave her.

The beauty of trials is that in them we see what the true reward and glory is: knowing God Himself. It is no surprise that in the letter Paul wrote to the church in Ephesus there is mention of this along with gearing up for warfare. He writes, "I pray that you, being rooted and established in love, may have power, together with all the saints, to grasp how wide and long and high and deep is the love of Christ, and to know this love that surpasses knowledge—that you may be filled to the measure of all the fullness of God" (Ephesians 3:17–19), and then in chapter 6 he tells how to put on the armor of God to fight off the attacks of the enemy. We must grasp that, though these attacks come, they produce a great reward. Just as Romans 5 highlights, trials produce perseverance, which produces our character, which in turn produces hope. That hope is in Christ, and that hope makes every tear worth it, my friends. That hope makes even lying in your closet curled in a ball copiously sobbing worth it, for we will get more of Him.

Typically, if the enemy is attacking you, God has something really incredible happening behind the scenes. Don't cave. Don't walk away. Press into Him, for as it says in Psalm 91:4, "Under his wings you will find refuge." He is glorified when we admit our own weakness and how desperately we need Him. He is glorified when we come to know His character better through these trials. He is glorified when we are no longer distracted from mundane life, and are given the heavy coat of burden to wear for a time so that He can take it off of us. He is glorified, and we are satisfied in Him to the point where it is not the storm ending or the potential rewards at the end that we desire; it's knowing Him more truly.

Prayer

Dear Lord,

We praise You for this day. Lord, some reading this, including myself, are under attack today. We are scared and as ardently as we want to think that our strength is sufficient, we fall short of being able to save ourselves. We need a Savior; we need You. Lord, please be our shield and rampart. Lord, please overwhelm us with Your Holy Spirit. Cover us with Your wings, and bring us into a deeper understanding of who You are. You are the glory, Lord.

Bring us ever closer to You.

In Your name we pray,

Amen.

CHAPTER 8

Bloomed

COLLEGE

College. At long last you've moved your tassel to declare your independence from high school. Everyone is asking what you're doing next. Perhaps you're headed to a university, ready to conquer the world with your eighteen-year-old self. You have a hidden sense of confidence that you have achieved all you will ever need to know to be successful ahead, because after all you are legally an adult. Then comes the first day on campus.

It feels slightly like a flashback to kindergarten, where everyone is your age, but you know no one. The bigger kids are slightly intimidating, and you secretly want to hold on to your parents for dear life. It's okay; it's normal to feel this.

In our society, college has become almost a rite of passage. That is not to say that college is for everyone, because it's not, but for many people it is a necessary step depending on their career. College is an entirely new world full of possibilities and opportunities to learn more about yourself, God, and who God made you to be.

I remember first starting out at college. I began at Randolph-Macon College, which was not a Christian school. My parents had desired for me to go to college since they weren't able to, so I worked my little rear off to get into a good school. Randolph-Macon was not my first choice by a long shot. I tried to get into the University of Richmond, but God had different plans. Although I was disappointed, I sought to make the best of ol' Randy Mac. I was not prepared, nor did I expect what I found there.

Everything I believed in was challenged and questioned from day one. My adolescent childhood of *VeggieTales* and goodnight prayers was mocked as I stepped into the lion's den. Finding my own voice and questioning what I truly believed became a daily occurrence. It was easy to slip into the shadows at a school, yet a deep longing for companionship grew steadily.

One of my classes was designed to change the way students think, as the professors sought to challenge us regarding what we were taught growing up was the (literal) gospel truth. Some of the assignments were in good taste, an honest approach to break any social barriers of money or status. The most astounding finding was that everything in my life was now held in question. There were no Spark Notes or cheat codes; it was the real world.

Something that became very evident as well was the pressure of temptation. Though I'd been taught about this constantly throughout my childhood to keep me safe, now it became real. The access to alcohol and drugs was extremely easy, as was the desire to fit in.

It became evident that most of the students came to party, and party they did. I remember walking down the street on the third day of classes to find a girl passed out in a bed of flowers at 10 a.m. So where does this leave us? What is the line between living the right way and going too far?

In our lives, there is a constant balance of being in the world but not of it, which at times can make it feel impossible to figure out the sweet spot. Especially in college with all the temptations so easily fulfilled, it only adds to the potential for compromise. That is why it is important to take a good, hard look at yourself. Who are you? What do you believe? Do you believe that because your parents told you to, or because you have examined the evidence and found it to be true? If so, how are you going to defend it? This is also a good time to open the door of opportunity to ask questions and seek wise leaders who are doing well and have a good relationship with God, and watch them. Don't lose yourself trying to become someone you aren't. Together with God, figure out what is most important to you and what your goals are as a godly person. Spend these years discovering who you are, who God made you to be, and where you are going. Spend as much time as possible in the Word and in prayer. Not a moment of that will be squandered. Lastly, be open to your plans changing. Your life shouldn't be confined to what you *thought* was going to happen.

Dear Lord,
Thank You for the gift of learning. Lord, let us never become
wrapped up in the belief that education is a marker of success, but
let us hold firmly that education is to be used to understand You
and the world around us more. Let us do all things, including
school or trade, for Your glory.
In Jesus' name,
Amen.

FAILURE TO LAUNCH: JOBS

Remember career day in kindergarten where you got to portray what you wanted to be when you grew up? At the time, it was a fun activity, but I didn't realize that it would be a precedent for what the remainder of my schooling would pertain to: what I wanted to be as an adult.

Of course, we rarely know at age five what we want to spend the remaining seventy-five years of our lives doing, but it did get the ball rolling on thinking about it. High school became the pressing period to get into a good college, which would secure a good job, which would secure a good life. An avalanche of pressure began rolling with the small snowball of career day.

More than likely you said you wanted to be an astronaut or nurse at age five, but perhaps now you are thinking of something entirely different. In your final years of high school you may have no earthly idea, but in the midst of college you may have a firmer grasp on what you want to do. Believe it or not, people rarely end up in the profession of their major. According to the *Washington Post*, only 27 percent of college graduates ended up in a profession related to their major.[10]

Society and your environment can also positively or negatively affect your future plans. Perhaps a parent or mentor will suggest a "safe" major such as business that will more than likely secure a cubicle job by age twenty-five. Looking back, a good friend actually became a nurse because all the women in her family had been nurses for generations. Sometimes those closest to us mean well and earnestly want to impart wisdom to help us in our future ventures, but in the end, it is between you and God alone.

By nature, I am a planner. I can tell you what the remainder of my week looks like and I nearly have a virtual calendar in my head of my writing schedule for the next month. I am sadly not even joking. When it came to a career, though, I was totally lost. In high school, I thought for sure I wanted to be a museum curator. Being slightly (more than slightly) obsessed with the *National Treasure* franchise, the idea of working in a museum made my heart soar (as did Riley Poole, haha). I sought out a summer internship at a local museum and found that though it was a great summer job, it wasn't for me. College rolled about, and I changed my major multiple times. I decided on English because of a teacher I had in the tenth grade who changed every aspect of how I saw writing and literature; additionally, Don Henley of the Eagles had said being an English major helped him in songwriting. After college, I still pursued my writing and songwriting, but ended up selling and fixing phones and computers for Apple. Then health issues caused me to leave Apple and I worked as a teller for Wells Fargo . . . let's just say that was basically the place where creativity, dreams, and happiness go to die. Then God kind of hit me over the head with what He wanted me to do—what I had said twenty years prior at career day: teach.

The thing is, I could have saved a lot of time going for teaching years earlier, but I do not regret a single day at the other jobs. God used that time so well. Working for the museum taught me how to bring history alive to others. Apple took an extremely introverted girl and plunged her into the busiest retail store, and she grew. I learned how to talk to people, how to teach others how to use their products, and how to have a heart-to-heart connection with a stranger and step out talking about God sometimes too.

Wells Fargo taught me that I hate corporate, and that I am far too creative to be so stifled, but what it also allowed me to do was to write. I took my journal with me and scribbled down devotionals, chapters, ideas, and prayers throughout my day. I then sought out a few online publications to publish my devotionals and articles and was picked up by Polished Ministries to become the leader of their teen department. It also is what spurred me to begin writing this book.

God used every single job experience to prepare me for the next. When He led me to teach, nothing had ever felt so right. It all clicked, and just as with Elisha's servant in 2 Kings 6:17, God opened my eyes to see. The calling I ignored for twenty years ended up being the one thing that made me actually want to get up in the morning to do. It made me feel fulfilled and happy, even if I was making a small paycheck.

It may take years of random jobs to find what is exactly right for you, but each of those jobs is a stepping stone. Each job reveals more of what you enjoy doing, and what you don't enjoy doing. In many ways, "God blessed the broken road that led me straight to you" (my lovely job!).

As you're reading this you may be thinking either, *Yay! That's good news for me,* or, *Sure, that's great...for you* (eye roll). If it is the latter, that's okay. It is okay not to know what you want to do when you grow up. I don't think many adults know what they want to do when they grow up. Even praying about it for years may result in unanswered prayer and confusion, but fear not. God knows your heart so well that He knows exactly how to reveal His plan for you. He knows how you are wired, because He made you, and He knows how to get you to the right place.

If you're in school, try joining any club, group, or society that interests you. If nothing else, you will find a passion or a hobby, or will discover something that you hate. Sometimes what we stumble upon ends up becoming something we truly do love. I recall times in high school where I would express a dream or hope I had, only for it to be dashed by others. It was not that my aspirations were capricious, rather those around me held a bitter root because of a failed dream or missed opportunity in their own lives. Yet as sad as that is for them, it is not the sentence upon your own life. God has a specific story written solely for you, and that story does not belong to them. Consider how snowflakes are all uniquely different, each with its own individual design. One snowflake does not worry itself with what another snowflake's design looks like, for it has its own pattern to live by. In the same way, we ought to be like snowflakes, living our individual life with our own unique, God-given purpose.

In the same way, do not let what others say dictate a career for your life. It is your life, and it's what you have to spend every day doing. Knowing you are doing exactly what you are supposed to do matters more than what is in the bank. We are convinced so often that to be successful our bank accounts should be bloated and our tangible possessions of high value. Yet at the end of our lives we will care about the impact we made, the memories we formed, and the life we created far more than the dollars left in the bank. If you can go to bed at night knowing you have satisfied what the Lord had for you to do that day, then the scoffs and opinions of others should hold no real importance, nor should the dollars in the bank.

Ultimately be fueled by what you know you are here to steward and carry out in this life. God created you with a specific purpose, specific calling, and specific mission in your life, but it is up to you to embrace that calling or shove it away. We spend so much of our lives trying to please the people around us when doing so leaves us miserable. Your value is not contingent upon the opinions of others. Partner with the Lord for what you are called to do on this earth and make the commitment to God and yourself that you will not compromise that mission. For what is on this earth is as fleeting as the wind, but the expeditions we carry out with God are eternal.

Prayer

Dear Lord,
You know all things, most especially the hearts
You have grown in us. Lord, please guide our decisions and
teach us to fully trust You, even when we do not see how or
when or why. Lord, make our paths straight and direct us
so that we in turn understand You more deeply.
In Jesus' name,
Amen.

MENTORING THOSE YOUNGER THAN YOU

There comes a true blessing in helping other people, and as Christians we are called to do so. This includes mentoring those younger than us. Often the word "mentor" holds the connotation of someone over age sixty taking long walks in the park to share wisdom, but in truth, it's befriending someone younger than you and sharing lessons you've learned.

Everyone has a story, everyone has learned something in their lives, and everyone can stand to learn from others. Not a single person on earth has learned everything or seen everything, and often they can save a lot of trouble if they learn from others.

It's one thing to understand that it is important to mentor, but it's another to find someone to mentor. Of course, it is important to pray for guidance, but there are other ways to find a mentoring relationship. For example, volunteer with the youth at church, in clubs like Big Brothers/Big Sisters, or in Scouts. Even if you do not think you have something to offer, dollars to donuts something you've been through could help someone else.

The personal element is becoming harder to find in a world built around technology, but that makes it all the more vital. We must not allow technology to steal the true essence of what our hearts are made for.

Our Creator said that it is not good for man to be alone (Genesis 2:18), and as such we need each other. We need others to learn from, to grow from, and to help. Mentoring is a beautiful ministry that embraces this, but also changes us in the process. Throughout the Scriptures we see examples of this, such as Elijah mentoring Elisha, Moses mentoring Joshua, Paul mentoring Timothy, and Jesus mentoring the disciples.

God often works in mysterious ways to provide someone to mentor you, or for you to mentor someone else. Prayer is the key, along with discernment. A wise man once said to never take advice from someone doing worse than you, and there is much truth in that statement. Being mentored is important in that you test each and every ounce of what a person is saying against the Word of God to ensure that it is indeed of Him. In the same way, whatever you are sharing with someone you mentor should be checked according to the will of God and His Word.

Go forward and pray for a mentor or someone to mentor. Don't shy away from it; embrace it and flourish from it.

Prayer

Dear Lord,
We thank You for mentors and for those to mentor.
Lord, just as You matched those in the Bible for such callings,
we pray You would do the same today in us.
In Jesus' name,
Amen.

HANGING IN THERE ALONG THE WAY

Do you keep a personal journal? Journals differ from most mediums we use to chronicle time in that they are so personal. Pictures provide a snapshot of the highlights of life, whereas journals can capture the lowlights. Because within journals the inner struggles, the unsure emotions, and the truthful revelations of life can abide freely. There is not a fear that these words will be exposed to the outside world, and therefore raw honesty can flow. In reading my own journals I gained strength in seeing how the girl I once was found her path to hang in there along the way.

There is so much more to the journey than just trudging through the muck of life. There will be times that the path requires going through a difficulty rather than around it, but there is never a place that does not hold purpose or intentionality for your future. Consider how the nation of Israel did not avoid the Red Sea, but rather walked through it. That adds to the truth of how in our own struggles we can make the choice of what our perspective will be during the journey. There arises the question, what is God doing in this part of the story? We so often get wrapped up in the moment that we neglect to consider what this leg of the journey is attempting to teach us, grow in us, or lead us to.

God cares more about the growth and development of our heart, character, and spiritual life than about our productivity. It is also important to Him how we are responding to the hurdles life will throw at us. Where are we placing our hope and what are we setting our eyes on?

One of the most important ways of responding to life's issues is to connect with the Lord through prayer. Our lives matter to Him, and He actually invites us with a wide open door to come to Him with our issues. Through prayer we can come before

Him with our vulnerable hearts in sharing how we feel about something. It is not like He doesn't already know, and it is in coming before Him that we can bear our burdens as well as receive peace, grace, and answers. Consider how Elijah heard God in that "gentle whisper" (1 Kings 19:12) and found the strength and peace he needed to hang in there.

Take into account what the outcomes have been in biblical scenarios as well. In 1 Samuel 21:9 David found himself in a seemingly unbearable place, one where he felt unsure of what to do next. God met him there in that struggle through a circumstance which would be truly laughable to call a mere coincidence. David was on the run hiding from Saul (more likely than not we have not found ourselves literally on the run for our lives from another person). David journeyed to the town of Nob to see Ahimelech the priest and asked if any weapon was there. The response he received was not just about the physical spear or sword he was hoping for, but something more significant. The sole weapon available for him was the sword of Goliath the Philistine, whom David had defeated as a teen, marking a solid victory in his life. From this look to the past and the victory God had brought forth through David, he found regained strength for the present battle.

Recall what God has done in and through you in the past, and ponder how that can be applied to your current situation. This can be where journaling your honest feelings and truths can show where you were so you can then see what the outcome was. Even in the seeming failures or events where others sought to bring you down, contemplate how a new path was forged that took you somewhere better than you could have ever imagined. Just as it says in Genesis 50:20, "You intended to harm me, but God intended it for good to accomplish what is now being done, the saving of many lives." People can attempt to push us down, but ultimately God is the one in charge of our lives, and through

His hand in our circumstances we can see situations changed for good. Don't judge the ending of the movie based on what it looks like thirty minutes in.

Share your life with those around you as well. This is where godly counsel is so vital in authentically doing life with others. Again, God said that it is not good for man to be alone, and therefore man was not meant to do life alone. We need each other for the good times *and* the bad. This is where sharing vulnerably can result in opportunities for support. I cannot begin to tell you how often I will be having a hard day and reach out to one of my Spirit sisters, and they come alongside me with a word of encouragement, a kind prayer, or a listening ear. They often bring ideas that I had not thought of as well. God loves to use His children as vessels to speak life and wisdom into situations, so invite others into the day to day, the questions, and the wonderings.

The more we continue in the path it becomes evident that by hanging in there, our weak muscles grow strong and we are changed along the way. We hold the choice to let what life throws at us make us better or bitter, and we also hold the choice to view the hardships as places that ruin us or places that open a doorway for us to become the people we were meant to be. Are you going to allow those hard times to leave you shattered, or are you going to pick up the pieces *with* God and allow Him to make a new masterpiece mosaic out of your life? Don't stray from your sincere and genuine words during this time, and also do not forget how God used those sufferings for something greater along the way.

WALK FEARLESSLY INTO THE FUTURE

"Fear not" is spoken in the Bible three hundred and sixty-five times, and as the saying goes, we should refrain from becoming afraid every day of the year. However, this is far easier said than done. Fear is inevitable in our lives; no matter how earnestly we try to become Spartans and tough as nails, at some point will fall prey to fear. But when we do, we have an advocate behind us.

What does it really mean when we are afraid? First John 4:18 says, "There is no fear in love. But perfect love drives out fear, because fear has to do with punishment. The one who fears is not made perfect in love." So, when we don't feel loved, we feel afraid. We fear that God no longer loves us, or really, God no longer likes us, and we become fearful of the unknown. This is no surprise to Christ. He knows we are human and that at times we will not feel that perfect love and be subject to fear. What are we to do about this problem then? First Peter 5:7 shares, "Cast all your anxiety on him because he cares for you." This is easy to say, but what does it really mean? The act of casting out our fears is very much like casting a net out for fish; it won't always bring all we need on the first try. We must cast out these fears again and again and reel in the peace each time the enemy comes knocking with that fear. Trust that in the course of doing so, we are not merely reaping peace but are coming to actually understand Him better.

Jesus wants to take on your problems. Really, He does. He says so in Matthew 11:28–30: "Come to me, all you who are weary and burdened, and I will give you rest. Take my yoke upon you and learn from me, for I am gentle and humble in heart, and you will find rest for your souls. For my yoke is easy and my burden is light." He actually desires to take on your burdens and walk with you through those dark times. The beauty is that when we are walking through those storms with Him, we actually begin to see the light and we feel that peace; we feel loved. That love translates in our hearts and soothes the fears, bringing to truth that indeed perfect love casts out all fear. Perhaps that is the "beauty from ashes" that comes from fears that rock us to our core; we come to find the true meaning of love and peace in Christ.

How then can we walk without fear into the future? Proverbs 31:25 is another coffee mug verse that shares, "She is clothed with strength and dignity; she can laugh at the days to come." Another translation gives the more literal meaning: "Strength and honor are her clothing; she shall rejoice in time to come" (NKJV). Now, laugh and rejoice are very distinct here. What is being conveyed is that, because she knows the origin of her strength and hope, she can rejoice in the days to come. Yes, there will be difficult days ahead, but in holding firm to that faith in God, we can walk fearlessly into the future. We can declare with the utmost confidence that we are no longer slaves to fear, for we are children of God and can dive deep into that perfect love.

A woman who rejoices in the days to come stands differently than those around her. She does not limit herself to the small scope of what she sees, for she knows there are far more things in action than what she can understand in this passing moment. She resolves to believe with everything in her that her days are planned out before her, and that indeed all things will come together for good and the glory of God. When we walk in this truth, we no longer become consumed by the discouragement of the world. Some may consider this mindset escapism or extreme optimism, but perhaps it is actually tapping into the truthful reality of what God has for us, rather than the defeating perspective that the dark forces of this world would like to convince us of.

Dear Lord,
We know fear is not from You, and we pray that Your perfect love
would cast out all fear we have. We pray that You would cleanse
us and guide us in the way that we should go, fearlessly into the

future. We pray that You would overwhelm us with Your peace
that goes beyond all understanding.
In Jesus' name,
Amen.

I JUST CAN'T WAIT TO BE KING

One of my all-time favorite movies is *The Lion King,* and one of the most memorable scenes is where Simba as a cub is singing about how he cannot wait until he is grown and able to become king. Isn't that true of all of us? Makes me think of when I was a young teen, so excited to drive, have a bank account, get a job, and make real money—all to find that once I stepped into that adult reality, I wanted to revert back.

Growing up has so many perks and freedoms, like driving and the ability to make decisions for yourself, but at the end of the day, it really does come back to the need for guidance. You can be seventeen or seventy-seven, but you still need guidance. This is where the Lord really does become your best friend yet again.

There's a verse in Jeremiah where the Lord says, "Stand at the crossroads and look; ask for the ancient paths, ask where the good way is, and walk in it, and you will find rest for your souls" (Jeremiah 6:16). God brought this verse to mind when I was praying about teaching, actually. This verse rings such truth. If you note, it mentions the ancient paths, so this reminds us that we are not the first ones to question what path to take. It's almost a beautiful burden knowing how many options we have and paths we could take these days.

So, to keep this short and sweet: ask God. Ask God, and follow His path. It may be scenic, it may require daring faith, it may appear completely impossible, but following Him is never a bad idea. Faithfulness is always rewarded, just not necessarily on our timelines. But He is faithful, and He has a plan. You will end up being glad to be you in the end.

Scenic routes are not to be considered the less desirable of journeys either. Typically, when setting out on a trip we ask Siri or Alexa to direct us in the fastest way, avoiding backroads and preferring highway travel. Yet many times in our lives the Lord will instead take us in a way that is off the well-traveled highways. There are benefits such as avoiding heavy traffic, roadway collisions, or road blocks. The scenic route seemingly takes longer, but along the way we see prairies and fields, vast beautiful forests, and mountain-view overlooks. The destination is not the only prize to be sought; the journey there holds just as much value, if not more. Don't forgo the benefits of a scenic route. Don't fall prey to having a dampened attitude, sulking down the journey's road. Don't merely focus with selective vision on what is occurring around you, for there is far more happening than what is directly in front of you. Lastly, recall that you were chosen to embark on this way for a reason. The scenic route might just be the tale you love to tell one day to future adventurers. Onward!

CHAPTER 9

The One

AT LAST

"You're too picky. This is a nice Christian boy; you should be with him."

"What are you waiting for? Just choose a guy and go for it."

"Your ideals are too high. God doesn't care who you marry."

Lies. All of these are ideas that our society, completely obsessed with instant gratification, gravitates toward. I cannot even begin to tell you how many weddings I have attended where the bride and groom seem to be marrying after a knee-jerk reaction with crossed fingers that they were making the right decision. What if instead of grabbing the first spouse we can get, like a sweater on Black Friday that you later regret, we take a step back? What if we are patient and we, wait for it, let God choose? What if He does care about our lives—including our love lives—and we let Him take the lead? What if we stop fearing waiting? What if there really is a moment where everything comes to a forefront and we at last see who He has for us? Stick with me here.

In all of human history there has been only one perfect

marriage, well…perfect for a time. You see, the first marriage was between Adam and Eve, and before that dirty rotten serpent showed up, everything in the garden was perfect. That means that their marriage, instituted by God, was also perfect. The truth is God designed man not to be alone, and the vast majority of people He designed for marriage. Now of course there is the very vital and pertinent aspect of what a godly and healthy marriage looks like with God as the head, but let's just focus on the beginning.

> The LORD God placed the man in the Garden of Eden to tend and watch over it. But the LORD God warned him, "You may freely eat the fruit of every tree in the garden—except the tree of the knowledge of good and evil. If you eat its fruit, you are sure to die."
>
> Then the LORD God said, "It is not good for the man to be alone. I will make a helper who is just right for him." So the LORD God formed from the ground all the wild animals and all the birds of the sky. He brought them to the man to see what he would call them, and the man chose a name for each one. He gave names to all the livestock, all the birds of the sky, and all the wild animals. But still there was no helper just right for him.
>
> So the LORD God caused the man to fall into a deep sleep. While the man slept, the LORD God took out one of the man's ribs and closed up the opening. Then the LORD God made a woman from the rib, and he brought her to the man.
>
> "At last!" the man exclaimed.
> "This one is bone from my bone,
> and flesh from my flesh!
> She will be called 'woman,'
> because she was taken from 'man.'"

This explains why a man leaves his father and mother and is joined to his wife, and the two are united into one.

Now the man and his wife were both naked, but they felt no shame. (Genesis 2:15–25, NLT)

There is a lot here to chew on, so let's start chomping. God makes Adam, and He sees that it is not good for him to be alone. From the start, we see that mankind is made to be in relationship with God and with each other. God makes every animal and asks Adam to name them all. Adam seems pretty content in this perfect paradise of a garden, a bachelor pad of sorts, along with all the animals. He has a perfect relationship with God, yet there is still something that God says needs to be added. All the animals have mates, but man does not. Adam needs a wife.

Let's take a moment to consider the intentionality of God in the construction of Eve as well. He could have scooped up in His hands the dust of the earth to form Eve as He did Adam, but instead He forms Eve from part of Adam, his rib to be precise. A rib has many functions in the body, but primarily it serves three purposes. First, the ribs help to hold the body upright so that it not slump, collapse, or fall over. Think about how a wife can serve that role in marriage as well. Secondly, the ribs assist the lungs in breathing. Ribs move up and down as you breathe to create the space the lungs need to expand and collapse. Lastly, the ribs protect the organs in the thoracic cavity, including the heart. The heart is protected—and could there be a lovelier comparison to a wife protecting the heart of her husband? God is such a poet, and His intentions are never without meaning. Eve was made in such a way that she may bless her husband in more ways than merely being a companion.

So, in the course of this surgery, Adam naps. Then God brings the woman to Adam and wakes him up. What does Adam say the first time he sees his wife? Is it, "Oh, well, this chick is here and it's good enough I guess." NO! He says, "At last!" Ladies, swoon over this—imagine if your future spouse was so focused on God and willing to wait that when God finally revealed you he would look at you and say, "At last!" Now, wouldn't that be worth the wait? Wouldn't that be something sustaining and beautiful to hold out for?

When this story occurs, their union is holy. Sacred. Perfect. God designed every single aspect of this union, and He will do that with your love story if you let Him. Stop taking the first exit you see and let God drive. Be so focused on God and all He has called you to that until He says it is time for you to wake up, you'll keep trusting Him. You will keep focused on Him and the things He has asked you to do in the meantime—even if it is literally naming animals. When the time is right, He will reveal it, and your heart and all of heaven will rejoice in proclaiming, "At last!"

Prayer

Dear Lord,
We praise You for Your time spent on us, knowing us through and through as You speak about in Psalm 139. Lord, we pray that just as You know our hearts, You would highlight to us when the time is right for our very own "at last!" moment. We pray that this moment would be eye-opening, but most truly gloriously praising to You above all else.
In Jesus' name,
Amen.

BONE FROM MY BONE

What did Adam mean in the passage above where he called Eve "bone from my bone"? Again, Genesis 2:23 says,

"This one is bone from my bone,
and flesh from my flesh!
She will be called 'woman,'
because she was taken from 'man.'"

Perhaps what he was saying was that she was his people. In today's terms, we might say that we've found our "lobster" (our lifelong mate, according to *Friends*). I love the imagery given in Isaiah 34: "None of these will be missing, not one will lack her mate. For it is his mouth that has given the order, and his Spirit will gather them together." God is the one who brings these people together, not man. Adam knew this without a doubt. God tells us, "Call to me and I will answer you and tell you great and unsearchable things you do not know" (Jeremiah 33:3). That is what happened here; God showed Adam something great, all right. Adam knew immediately that this woman standing before him was the one. She would be cut from the same cloth. In modern terms, she might be the one who would obsess over *Star Wars* with him, watch football games, talk about conspiracy theories for hours on end, and get McDonald's at midnight with him just for fun. She would be his, and he would be hers. Isn't this a beautiful thought? A beautiful hope? A beautiful desire for God to fulfill?

Now, this is not to say that God was not or is not enough for each of us, because He is. He always is more than enough, but we must recall that God said it was not good that man was alone, and that is why He made a helper suitable for him. God made man and woman for Himself and then for each other. When those two things are in the proper order, that is where abundance is the atmosphere of the garden.

The more we dive into the Bible and stop to soak in the beautiful language of it all, the more we come to see that it is a beautiful representation of His love over us. God is the Author of all these words, and we can see those words carried out in our own lives.

"Bone from my bone" will look different for everyone. For some it may be as simple as shared interest in puns or movies or a sport. Let your walls down and you may just come to find that in fact God has more than you knew you ever wanted right there. Waiting all along for you.

―――――― *Prayer* ――――――

Dear Lord,
We praise Your holy name. We thank You for our quirks and
enigmatic tendencies, and Lord we pray that You would help us
to rejoice in those beautiful rarities in our spouses. Lord, we know
that no two snowflakes are alike, just as no two people are alike.
We thank You for such truths, and we pray that we rejoice in
those one-of-a-kind moments.
In Jesus' name,
Amen.

WHAT TO LOOK FOR IN A MAN

The list. Oh, the list, the list, the list. For as long as I can remember as a teen and beyond, there have been suggestions of a list of qualities to pray for in a husband. Oh sure, we start these lists around age thirteen and we say the canned answers we think we should write, but then we slip in or secretly hope he also has deep eyes. We secretly hope he's got strong arms to defend us. We secretly hope he looks like Steve Rogers from *Captain America* (oh wait, that's just me). The thing is, it is good to know what you want, but it's even better for God to show you. Let's go a little deeper to what that all means.

God made your heart. He said to the prophet Samuel,

"Do not consider his appearance or his height, for I have rejected him. The LORD does not look at the things man looks at. Man looks at the outward appearance, but the LORD looks at the heart." (1 Samuel 16:7)

God knows you. He knows you best, because He made you. Let that really fill up your mind, that God made y-o-u. He therefore knows what makes you happy, He knows what will be difficult for you, He knows the things you don't even know you want. All that being said, trust Him on the spouse front. We should dive into the Word to find traits to look for in a spouse—traits like honesty, a godly leader, a man after God's own heart—but let Him surprise you with other little idiosyncrasies. Make your list an outline of what a man after God's heart is, and then let Him fill in the extra lines. He knows your heart, and He won't leave you disappointed. Isaiah 49:23 says, "Then you will know that I am the LORD; those who hope in me will not be disappointed." God won't let you down or leave you high and dry. He knows your desires, and He knows what you need most.

In the same way, we should strive to be the kind of women who honor God most. If we desire a husband who is God's highest and best, shouldn't they be receiving a wife who is God's highest and best too? How do we do this?

For starters, we work to become the Proverbs 31 woman, not for our husbands, but for God. We are women created by and for Almighty God, and our days walking this earth are not in vain. So it is vital that we live out each and every day in His glory. Spend time in prayer and meditation over what being a Proverbs 31 kind of woman for God looks like now. Don't let this day be in vain.

Dear Lord,
Thank You for brains that can discern what is right and wrong.
Lord, please mold our hearts to Your will for our lives so that we
may in turn glorify You. Mold us to desire what You desire for us,
especially in men. Lord, guide our hearts, minds, spirits, and eyes
to see what You see.
In Jesus' name,
Amen.

ALL THE FEELS

There are places where the church needs to improve its approach to topics, and one of those truthfully is sex. Ephesians calls for husbands and wives to submit to each other, always looking out for the best interest of the other in love. It says in Song of Solomon to "not to awaken love until the time is right" (2:7, NLT), and we must hold very firmly to this. The most important aspect of this is taking it to God, not allowing anything to get out of hand. You are not a body with a soul, you are a soul with a body. Our bodies by design have carnal desires. However, we have a soul that dictates the actions of our body and we are responsible for those choices. This free will of the soul is intended to fulfill and honor the will of the One who made it. When we leave all our desires at the foot of the cross, He will help us to navigate these desires. Proverbs 21:1 says, "The king's heart is in the hand of the LORD; he directs it like a watercourse wherever he pleases," and Isaiah 48:17 states, "I am the LORD your God, who teaches you what is best for you, who directs you in the way you should go."

We live in a fallen world, so it is evident that indeed we will fall short at times. Temptations will come. It is more common for men to be the ones to struggle with temptations, but it is a common issue for women too. It's obvious that we cannot do life on our own accord. Without the Lord's help to withstand temptation, we are not above falling into sin. But after marriage, it is not only right to have such feelings of desire for our spouse, it was commanded by God when He told them to go and be fruitful and make little children who would honor Him too (Genesis 1:22). From the very start it was His intention that we embrace such feelings and in the context of marriage enjoy them. The entire book of Song of Solomon is based upon this. Do not feel discouraged by what the culture pushes in regard to sex; instead, go directly to the Word, the undying, Absolute Truth of God for what He intends for such feelings.

Prayer

Dear Lord,
Like a river, You can determine the course of a man's heart. Lord,
please direct our hearts, minds, and spirits according to Your will.
Lord, let us richly and deeply feel what You desire for us to feel so
that we may experience the fullness of Your plans for us.
In Jesus' name,
Amen.

EPILOGUE

So where do we go from here? What is next on the agenda? After you leave this little coffee sesh, what are you going to do? Here is what I suggest for all of us.

We live radically. We live in such a way that others see Jesus through us. We choose to not merely fall victim to the pitfalls of society, or to the gaps in church culture logic, but we live each and every day in such a way that we pick up our cross daily and follow Him.

This requires obedience, but as it says in 1 Samuel 15:22, "To obey is better than sacrifice." This requires being unpopular at times, and perhaps even losing friends. Jesus knew this, and in John 15:18–19 shares, "If the world hates you, keep in mind that it hated me first. If you belonged to the world, it would love you as its own. As it is, you do not belong to the world, but I have chosen you out of the world. That is why the world hates you." He has chosen you out of this world, so when you are rejected by the world do not see being a Christian as a mark of shame but as a badge of honor. Know that He has greater plans for you than what you may even think, for those plans are of His eternal Kingdom. What a beautiful thing when our efforts pour into the enduring glory of the Kingdom, and what an honor to be a part of such a duty.

Stand tall, stand firm, and stand out for Christ. Start each day knowing the God who holds the universe is holding on to you and holding your story in His hands.

No matter what life throws at you, hang in there, girl, you've got this. More importantly, He's got you.

NOTES

1. James E. McEldowney, "My Visit With Mahatma Gandhi" <web.archive.org/web/20210328011736/http://people. virginia.edu/~pm9k/jem/words/gandhi.html>.
2. "Religion," Dictionary.com.
3. C. S. Lewis, "Letter to Father Peter Bide," April 29, 1959, *The Collected Letters of C. S. Lewis*, Vol. 3.
4. "Let It All Out," lyrics by Matthew Thiessen, © Universal Music Publishing Group.
5. "Be My Escape," lyrics by Matthew Thiessen, © Universal Music Publishing Group.
6. Angela Thomas, *A Beautiful Offering* (Nashville TN: Thomas Nelson, 2006), 157–159.
7. C. S. Lewis, *Mere Christianity* (New York: Touchstone, 1996), 190–191.
8. John Piper, "Is Oral Sex Okay?" DesiringGod.com <desiringgod.org/interviews/is-oral-sex-okay>.
9. C. S. Lewis, *Letters of C. S. Lewis* (New York: Harper Collins Publishers, 1966), 317.
10. Brad Plumer, "Only 27 Percent of College Grads Have a Job Related to Their Major," *Washington Post*, May 20, 2013.

ACKNOWLEDGMENTS

In loving memory of Anna Reinstein, a teacher who helped me see the joy of writing. She changed my life, and I will be forever grateful.

Julia Brain, you are a gift to me not only as a friend and collaborator, but truly are a sister to me. Thank you for always helping me feel seen, known, loved, and understood. I treasure you.

A special thank you to Haley Wilging: You are more of a sister than I could have ever asked for, and I praise our Lord for you every single day.

Thank you to Shannon Lord, for standing with me and doing life with me. You inspire me to live authentically and sincerely without fear. You truly live up to your nickname "Shining On for the Lord," and I am so immensely thankful for you.

Melissa Eadie, thank you for being such a gem on a daily basis and a true friend. I am thankful to navigate with you all these crazy adventures He is writing for each of us.

To Gordon, my brother and adventure buddy in this life, I'm grateful for you and for the man God is growing you to be.

And to my wonderful parents, Glen and Maria, thank you for loving me, supporting me, and rooting for me all my life. I am so in awe of who you are as people, and so truly thankful to call you my mom and dad.

Lastly, to the man I will one day call my husband: May you know that you are richly loved by our Lord, and my heart awaits with eager expectation the day we are *at last* together.

Cally Logan is a US History teacher and Senior Writer for Crosswalk.com. She served as a small group leader for high school girls for several years, and enjoys challenging students to develop deeper relationships with God and to live fearlessly and authentically. She received her B.A. Degree from Regent University. In her spare time, she enjoys spending time in nature, genuine connection chats over coffee, and woodworking.

"In life, be a snowflake—leave a mark, but no stain."

TikTok: Cally_Logan
Instagram: CallyLogan
Twitter: CallyLogan

HELD
Melissa Eadie

Melissa Eadie was first diagnosed with cancer at the tender age of 14. While her peers were experiencing high school, the latest trends, and youthful ambitions, Melissa became familiar with the four corners of her hospital room. For the next 10+ years, "cancer," was a part of her everyday vocabulary. Tragically, her second diagnosis at 19 resulted in the loss of her right leg. A two-time cancer survivor and above knee amputee, Melissa's life is the definition of strength and perseverance, but she knows that victory includes the painful fight to the finish line. More than just a memoir, Melissa walks you through her vulnerable, "diary" moments in the process of growth, grieving, and forgiveness. Her story will lead you to the God that wraps you in love and shows you what it means to be ... Held.

ISBN: 978-1-61036-265-8

Instagram.com/@MellyDoesLife

BEAUTY FROM ASHES
Donna Sparks

In a transparent and powerful manner, the author reveals how the Lord took her from the ashes of a life devastated by failed relationships and destructive behavior to bring her into a beautiful and powerful relationship with Him. The author encourages others to allow the Lord to do the same for them.

Donna Sparks is an Assemblies of God evangelist who travels widely to speak at women's conferences and retreats. She lives in Tennessee.

www.story-of-grace.com

www.facebook.com/
   donnasparksministries/

www.facebook.com/
   AuthorDonnaSparks/

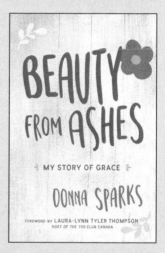

ISBN: 978-1-61036-252-8

FEARLESS
Angela Donadio

What do Jochebed, Rahab, Abigail, the woman at the well, the woman with the issue of blood, and Priscilla have in common? Find your fearlessness in their stories.

This 6-session Bible study will help you to:

Stand Up / Develop God-confidence to step into your unique calling.

Stand Out / Seize God-moments to make culture-shaping choices.

Stand Strong / Embrace God-sized dreams to become a catalyst for change.

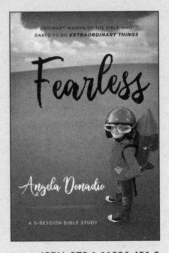

Readers will find their fearless in the inspiring stories of ordinary women of the Bible who dared to do extraordinary things.

www.angeladonadio.com

ISBN: 978-1-61036-401-0

BRIDGE
LOGOS